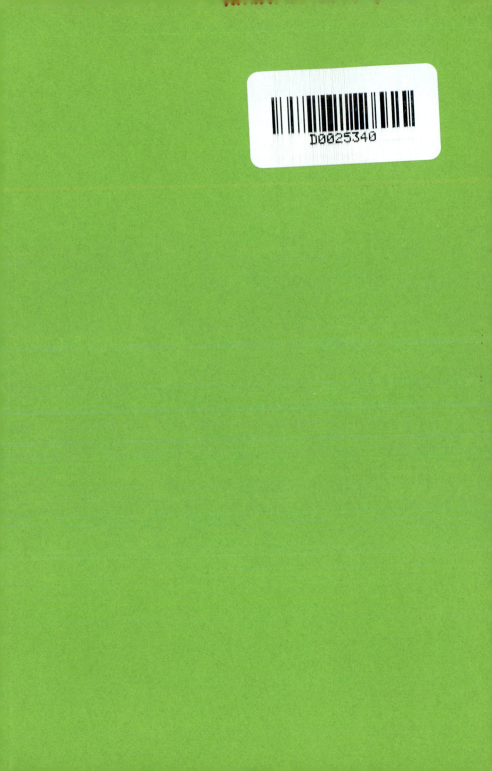

THE MALIGNED STATES
Policy Accomplishments, Problems, and Opportunities

POLICY IMPACT AND POLITICAL CHANGE IN AMERICA
Kenneth M. Dolbeare, Consulting Editor

Designed as brief supplements for American government and other undergraduate political science courses, books in this series confront crucial issues of public policy in the United States. The primary goal of the series is to demonstrate the utility of analytical concepts of political science for understanding the most pressing social and political problems of our time. Some books will be addressed to the question of how adequate present policies are to cope with current problems, and others will deal with questions of political change. Each book will be published in both soft- and cloth-cover editions.

Other books by Ira Sharkansky:

Spending in the American States
The Politics of Taxing and Spending
Regionalism in American Politics
Policy Analysis in Political Science
Public Administration: Policy-Making in Government Agencies
The Routines of Politics
State and Urban Politics: Readings in Comparative Public Policy
    (with Richard I. Hofferbert)
Urban Politics and Public Policy
    (with Robert L. Lineberry)
Politics and Policy in American Governments
    (with Donald Van Meter)
The United States: A Study of a Developing Country

THE MALIGNED STATES
Policy Accomplishments, Problems, and Opportunities

Second Edition

Ira Sharkansky

Department of Political Science
The Hebrew University of Jerusalem
and The University of Wisconsin-Madison

McGRAW-HILL BOOK COMPANY

New York   St. Louis   San Francisco   Auckland   Bogotá   Düsseldorf
Johannesburg   London   Madrid   Mexico   Montreal   New Delhi
Panama   Paris   São Paulo   Singapore   Sydney   Tokyo   Toronto

THE MALIGNED STATES: POLICY ACCOMPLISHMENTS, PROBLEMS, AND OPPORTUNITIES

1234567890 MUMU 783210987

This book was set in Press Roman by Creative Book Services, subsidiary of McGregor & Werner, Inc. The editors were Lyle Linder and Phyllis T. Dulan; the cover was designed by Rafael Hernandez; the production supervisor was Milton J. Heiberg.
The Murray Printing Company was printer and binder.

Library of Congress Cataloging in Publication Data

Sharkansky, Ira.
    The maligned states.

    (Policy impact and political change in America)
    Includes index.
    1. State governments. I. Title. II. Series.
JK2408.S46   1978   320.9'73'09 24   77-5703
ISBN 0-07-056434-5

FOR
TILLIE AND MORRIS MINES

Contents

Preface

When a scholar works persistently with a subject it is perhaps inevitable that he acquires an inordinate appreciation of its virtues. Much like the anthropologist who wants to protect "his" native village from the outside world, I have enlisted myself in the defense of state governments. In other publications I looked dispassionately at the states and used them for studying the politics and economics of policy making. While doing this work I came to feel that the states generally, and some poor states in particular, were treated unfairly by social scientists, journalists, and politicians. While others were writing that the states were the "fallen arch" in the federal system, I found evidence of their strength. This book contains some materials published earlier, but has new information now in a format that emphasizes the accomplishments and opportunities of the states in comparison with other levels of government. To be sure, there remain problems. Lethargic bureaucrats, backward politicians, and seemingly hopeless programs in individual states are seen along with fiscal strength and numerous signs of hope. In this book I emphasize material that shows the strength of state governments. I am not unaware of contrary arguments, and I deal with several that have the most credence. As I read the evidence about the strengths and weaknesses of the state governments, it says that we can—and must—count on state governments to service our most pressing social problems.

Much has happened in the United States since the first edition of *The Maligned States*. The country extracted itself from the longest war in its history and witnessed its first-ever resignation of a chief executive. The economy saw its most serious unemployment since the Depression, and its steepest inflation since World War II. Revenue sharing has established itself as a key ingredient of public finance, and New York City has teetered on the brink of bankruptcy, propped up more by the state than the national government.

The states remain viable beyond the 200th birthday of the country. Indeed, an extension of the financial analyses employed in the first edition shows that state governments have grown to further dominate the fields of policy that are jointly governed by themselves plus national and local units.

Any view of the states in 1977 must take account of several big and many small changes that have occurred since 1971. As I view these changes, they have not undermined the argument I made earlier. Accordingly, this revision is more an update than a reformulation. I have examined new data and fresh projections, pondered the events of the past years from the perspective of the states, and sought to improve the expression of many points called to my attention by perceptive readers.

As I write this preface to the second edition, the view from my study is not the lush green of Wisconsin but the mountains and valleys of Jerusalem. The government here is unitary in character, with traditions and problems that differ greatly from those of the United States. In revising this book I have resisted the temptation to compare the American states with governmental bodies elsewhere. Such comparisons might be made with profitable insights to politics and policy making. Yet it is also important to appreciate the role of the states in the American context, and that remains the mission of this book.

While I was writing this book initially, a small sign reinforced my intentions. Wisconsin had another election that focused on revenues, and the Democratic candidate won despite his "more taxes are necessary" side of the debate. A day after the election—and certainly unprodded by his parents—a seven-year-old penned this letter:

11/4/70

Dear Governor Lucey:
I don't want my Mommy and Daddy paying higher tax money.
We will get flat broke and I will not get any toys.

I'm mad at Mommy and Daddy voting for you. I wanted Jack Olson.

A Person Who Did Not Vote for You,
Stefan Sharkansky

With sentiments like this among the third-graders of America, the state governments need all the help they can get.

As its subtitle indicates, this book concerns the accomplishments, problems, and opportunities of state governments. Any definition of an accomplishment, problem, or opportunity depends on one's perspective. A liberal's accomplishment or opportunity is a conservative's problem. The perspectives behind this book are more eclectic than doctrinaire. The author's political philosophy might best be defined as "flexible," "pragmatic," or "peculiar." He sometimes joins liberals in applauding state government efforts to expand their roles to help the disadvantaged or to regulate private incursions against the public's welfare. At other times he has felt betrayed by sloppy or callous public administrators, by politicians who pursue support by simplistic programs and whose generosity is unmatched by serious planning or careful implementation, and by citizens who think government capable of solving all social problems. The author's judgments will lead inflexible liberals as well as hidebound conservatives to gnash their teeth at one time or another.

We cannot take lightly the task of evaluating state activities. Some states are more responsive than others to their citizens' needs or demands. The diversity that justifies the states' autonomy in a federal structure complicates any effort to judge them against a single standard of merit. Sharp differences in economic resources from one state to another introduce obvious barriers to equal performance. Some states do more than others with available resources. Tax rates vary. Several of the low-resource states collect and spend more revenue than several of the high-resource states. Within individual states there are differences in performance from one field of policy to another. Priorities vary widely and provide some of the clearest signs that ours is not a homogeneous culture. The residents of some states prefer lower taxes to improvements in services. By looking from one state to another, citizens can find outstanding programs in conservation, higher education, mental health, highway safety, or educational broadcasting. Chances are they will not find outstanding performance across this range in any one state. There are numerous problems in providing the complex services demanded by contemporary citizens. It is improbable that sufficient money, professional talent, and citizen-plus-official dedication will exist in any one jurisdiction to provide excellent services in all its programs.

Several institutions and individuals helped with this book. The Graduate Research Committee and the Center for the Study of Public Policy and Administration at the University of Wisconsin provided financial support for several empirical studies that started me thinking along these lines. Kenneth M. Dolbeare, Peter K. Eisenger, Brett W. Hawkins, Robert L. Lineberry, Faith Mote, Clara Penniman, Allan Rosenbaum, and Frances Hurst reviewed early drafts of the first edition. At a critical stage in the book's development, I profited from a brief visit with Daniel J. Elazar and his students and colleagues at the Center for the Study of Federalism at Temple University. Deanna Gervasi did the typing. Erica, Stefan, and Ina helped as usual. Of course, I assume the responsibility.

The dedication is for my grandparents. They contributed to this book over the course of many years, with numerous stories about the bad old days in Europe and America. With their recollections as my background, I could not help but feel uneasy with contemporary observers who malign the American states.

One pleasure in doing a new edition is the opportunity to accommodate the objections and suggestions of those readers who take the trouble to offer their remarks. This book has prompted much helpful correspondence and conversation since 1972. Rather than trying to cite personally all those who have contributed, I will limit myself to thanking here Robert R. Bezdek of Texas A & I University, William P. Angrick of Drake University, Thomas J. Pinckney of Austin Peay State University, and Richard D. Feld of East Texas State Univeristy who took the trouble to compile specific suggestions for this edition or who responded in detail to its first draft.

IRA SHARKANSKY

Chapter 1

Introduction

The states are powerful. Considering domestic public services only—and leaving out national defense and international relations—the states are growing in importance more than any other level of government. Since World War II the states have grown more than the national and local governments in their contributions to public services. After a heady 10 years of domestic innovations, international experiments with the Alliance for Progress, the war in Southeast Asia, and the excessive centralization of the national government's power in the White House, the Washington of the Ford administration became preoccupied with a tidy administration domestically and a strong, if not extended, position militarily. At the local level, city halls around the country scream poverty and look over their shoulders to the near bankruptcy of New York City. Meanwhile, the states have become more and more the workhorses rather than the weak sisters of the Federal system.

One of the ironies in American politics is that states reap so much negative publicity. Most public comments about the states say they are weak. That, indeed, is putting it mildly. They are said to be habitats of corrupt, evil, or simply ineffective politicians and bureaucrats. The states lack the image of innovation on the frontier of social and economic activity. The main political action seems to be in the cities and Washington. "States' Rights" conjures up the anachronisms of Klan members and backward programs in education, health, and welfare.

The states are maligned. They do not deserve to be the whipping posts of commentators who believe things should be better. Of course the society has problems. But the states are sources of strength. Many problems that are laid at the feet of state governments are actually the product of more complex forces. Those who say the future lies in the hands of the national and city governments should reexamine their heroes. The national government has produced severe social problems by the rigid and arbitrary procedures it imposes on the states. Local officials create many of their own difficulties by petty jealousies, a preference for competition rather than cooperation, and a reluctance to make tough decisions.

This book is *not* one more tirade against the states. Neither is it a defense of Klan members and backward social programs. It deals with the economic and political viability of the states and their central importance in the development and support of major public programs. Of course, the 50 states do not command equal praise. Like many of the stereotypes that social science must conquer, those dealing with the states have some accuracy. Yet the diversity in culture, economics, and politics is not simply unfortunate; state-to-state differences provide numerous pleasures and a continuing justification for the existence of distinct state governments. And there is some cause for joy even in those corners that deserve widespread scorn. Mississippi as well as New York provides salutary leadership in some fields of policy.

THE STATUS OF THE STATES

The days of glory for state governments appear to be long past. It was almost 200 years ago that James Madison described the states as having the greatest advantages of popular "predeliction and support." He compared the states to the Federal government and said:

> beyond doubt . . . the first and most natural attachment of the people will be to the governments of their respective states. Into

the administration of these a greater number of individuals will expect to rise. From the gift of these a greater number of offices and emoluments will flow. By the superintending case of these, all the more domestic and personal interest of the people will be regulated and provided for. With the affairs of these, the people will be more familiarly and minutely conversant.[1]

No prominent thinkers have defended the states in recent years. John C. Calhoun is the most recent advocate of the states who enjoyed national renown. His writing comes to us from the antebellum portion of the nineteenth century and describes a negative role for the states. Calhoun's principles of the concurrent majority and interposition are cited today by those who would have state governments nullify national actions that are obnoxious within state borders. When Orval Faubus called the Arkansas National Guard to block the integration of Little Rock Central High School and when George Wallace stood in the doorway of the University of Alabama they gave voice to the sentiments of Calhoun: that the decisions of a national majority should not be permitted to tyrannize contrary sentiments of state residents.

No government, based on the naked principle that the majority ought to govern, however true the maxim in its proper sense, and under proper restrictions, can preserve its liberty even for a single generation.... Affirm the right of the States, in their sovereign capacity, to decide, in the last resort, on the infraction of their rights and the remedy....[2]

Contemporary spokespersons for the states strike a negative pose before social progress. Too often, they see the strength of state institutions as guardians against unwanted change. Recent prominent advocates have included Lester Maddox and the late Senator Everett Dirksen. Maddox sought to protect his state from the integration guidelines of the U.S. Department of Health, Education, and Welfare. Dirksen took as his last great cause the passage of a constitutional amendment permitting *unequal* representation of voters in one house of each state legislature. During the period when he fought unsuccessfully for his amendment, the Senator observed that, "The only people interested in state boundaries will be Rand McNally."[3]

The inferior prestige of state governments is not a recent development. In 1933 a specialist in public administration wrote, "The

American State is finished. I do not predict that the States will go, but affirm that they have gone."[4] Professor Martin Landau traces what he considers to be the decline of the states:

> We have Woodrow Wilson's description, in 1885, of the "altered and declining status of the states." The pragmatic Frank Goodnow concludes in 1916 that industrialization has caused "the old distinction" between interstate and intrastate commerce "almost to disappear." And there is [Harold] Laski's tale of obsolescence and Max Lerner speaking of the ghost of federalism which "haunts a nation in which every force drives toward centralization." . . . Leonard White states "that competent observers at home and abroad have declared that American federalism is approaching its end." Roscoe Drummond put it more directly: "our federal system no longer exists."[5]

Landau's own view is an extension of this history:

> . . . the United States . . . has evolved into a highly centralized, integrated community. . . . It no longer possesses federal characteristics. . . . The United States has been for a long time now becoming the United State. . . .[6]

Landau is one of the observers who sees the frontier of social progress to be in relations between the national government and the cities. For him, Supreme Court decisions on the apportionment of state legislatures spelled the coup de grace of the Federal system. Nationally ordered reapportionment signaled the end of state control over its own political institutions. Also, it heightened the visibility of urban demands and strengthen the growing national-local axis. Now that the states cannot even define the composition of their own governments, it is about time to strike the final letter from United States. A contrary view of the Supreme Court's decisions—and the one adopted in this book—is that reapportionment has strengthened the states by increasing the likelihood that they will respond to their citizens' needs and demands. There is already some evidence of greater responsiveness that comes as a result of reapportionment. If the reapportionment decisions carried the look of a mortician when Landau published his essay in 1965, today they offer the promise of a physician.

The late professor Roscoe C. Martin argued forcefully that the great hope for social progress is with programs that unite the cities and the national government. In his view, states are "reluctant partners." They are in the way and discourage any serious effort at reform. Better to acknowledge and build upon the growing alliance of City Hall and Washington than to sink any great hopes in the modernization of state governments.

> That (the states) have been less than sensationally successful in coping with the problems of modern society would, perhaps, be generally conceded. . . .
>
> If a federal system, and specially the American system, is to function properly all members of the partnership must be strong and vigorous. It is a central conviction of this study that this precondition to success does not now obtain in America in that the states have not been able or willing to assume their share of federal responsibilities, particularly during the last three decades, and that the national government has been compelled to develop active relations with local governments in order to make the American system operationally effective.[7]

Martin wrote that a "state mind" embodies the features of provincialism and moral rigidity, plus outmoded support for the independent yeoman and weak government. His discussion of the state mind was totally without evidence. He provided no substantive information to indicate whether he was referring to the attitudes of state officials or to citizens' views of their state governments. He was certain, nonetheless, that the mind affects the nature of state policies:

> This state of mind and the myths growing from it have important consequences for state action. They result in a hard-bitten and almost uniform conservatism: what has been done over a period of years can continue to be done, but what is new and different must be regarded with suspicion.[8]

Martin believed that the state mind—and the state governments—are especially hostile to the cities:

> [To the state mind,] urban problems . . . spring from the unhealthy soil, even from the misdeeds, of the city. If the city is the

unnatural and unwanted issue of American growth, the difficulties that beset it lack the legitimacy of old-line claimants to public attention. Metropolitan problems are of the same genre; they are not matters with which the state need concern itself.[9]

Roscoe Martin and Martin Landau are not alone in their views about the need for a local-Federal axis. According to the mayors of two cities:

> Everything we've gotten in this city is from the Federal government. The state has not done one damned thing for us. . . .
>
> Our most satisfactory federal relations are with the departments which deal directly with the city. In the case of HEW, and some of the Labor Department programs, where we deal with Washington through the state capital, communications take six times as long.[10]

Even supporters of the state governments feel it necessary to operate from a defensive position. One of the few recent books written from the perspective of the state, by former Governor Terry Sanford of North Carolina, recognizes in its title that there is a *Storm over the States*. On the first page he starts with the admission:

> The states are indecisive.
>
> The states are antiquated.
>
> The states are timid and ineffective.
>
> The states are not willing to face their problems.
>
> The states are not responsive.
>
> The states are not interested in cities.
>
> These half-dozen charges are true about all of the states some of the time and some of the states all of the time.[11]

There is some evidence from survey research that the general public shares the antipathy toward the states that is expressed by so many intellectuals. When a random sample of American adults was asked how closely they follow different levels of government, the states came in fourth behind "national," "local," and "international." The people who pay attention mostly to the states have a distinctive set of traits that fit the stereotype of parochial citizens following anachronistic activities. Disproportionately, they grew up on farms, currently live outside of metropolitan areas, are Southerners, and have less than a high school education.[12]

The sharpest critics of state governments are the political liberals. They want government to *do things*, and they look for innovations in the national and local governments. Not the least of the states' problems is their image as the darling of the conservatives; "States' Rights" is the banner for those who would use government to halt social progress. For those who would recognize the progress that has come from the states and use the states to make more progress, there is a problem in establishing public credibility.

There is no getting around the fact that some states deserve a sordid reputation. What is objectionable—from the perspective of a well-balanced evaluation—is the tendency to overlook the commendable programs offered by many states. The tendency to lump all the states with the worst is now called the "Alabama syndrome." The label is a compliment to the status of George Wallace. The identification of all states with the worst has real consequences. When the equation is struck by legislative drafters, it means that all states are saddled with rigid procedures that inhibit creative policy making.

> In the drafting of the Economic Opportunity Act, an "Alabama syndrome" developed. Any suggestion within the poverty task force that the states be given a role in the administration of the act was met with the question, "Do you want to give that kind of power to George Wallace?" And so, in the bill submitted by President Johnson to Congress, not only George Wallace but Nelson Rockefeller and George Romney and Edmund Brown and all the other governors were excluded from any assigned role.[13]

THE ALLEGED PROBLEMS OF—AND WITH—STATE GOVERNMENTS

State authorities are blamed for permitting urban decay and the problems of poverty, ignorance, and crime that occur in the ghettos of large cities, and for the hopeless condition of the rural poor that produces migrants to the cities. It is said that the states have failed to develop programs of their own to alleviate the major social problems and have also restricted local governments from handling the problems that exist within their boundaries.

Those who see state governments as obsolete cite a number of problems with their basic structures and powers. Many of the state constitutions were drafted for conditions in the eighteenth and nineteenth centuries and appear inflexible in the face of contemporary needs.[14] The faults of being out-of-date are said to be:

1 State governments lack administrative integration and cannot pursue coherent action under the direction of the chief executive.

2 States have inadequate revenue powers that limit the revenue they can extract from economic resources lying within their jurisdictions.

3 States provide their local governments with outmoded financial aids that do not channel sufficient funds to areas of greatest need.

4 State constraints against local governments inhibit integrated, comprehensive metropolitan programs to deal with the social and economic problems in urban areas.

The single greatest problem that inhibits administrative integration in state government is said to be the weakness of governors. The chief executive is the single most prominent person in state politics, and the campaigns of those running for this office give the voters the one best opportunity to express their preferences for state policy. Yet the governor's control over the state's policy machinery seems meager. In most states a governor can appoint only a few of the top people in the bureaucracy. Important department heads are separately elected or named by multimember boards over which the governor has little control. Such key policy makers are not subject to the governor's power of removal and may not be tied even loosely to the governor by membership in a common political party. The voters of most states elect the attorney general and chief education officer. The result of popular elections for state department heads is not their dependence on the public so much as their *independence* from the governor. Without a dominant chief executive to impose policies on the relevant departments of the state bureaucracy, there is no central figure to push an integrated set of programs through the legislature or to implement authoritatively those programs that do exist. The officials of most states speak about "the governor's program." All too often, however, the governor merely lends his or her name to proposals that he or she passes unchanged from bureaucrats who design them to legislators who are asked to enact them. One study of state budgeting in Illinois talks about a governor who cannot cope with the machinery of state government. The conclusion applies to many other governors:

> The budget document may be compared to a huge mountain, which is constantly being pushed higher and higher by underground geological convulsions. On the top of the mountain is a single man, blindfolded, seeking to reduce the height of the mountain by dislodging pebbles with a teaspoon. That man is the Governor.[15]

The revenue provisions of many state constitutions are said to weaken their potential for successful programs. The taxes permitted by state constitutions are cited for two deficiencies. First, they are "regressive" in imposing heavier burdens on lower-income than on higher-income families. Second, state and local taxes are not sufficiently responsive to the prevailing inflationary trends and do not, therefore, provide sufficient levels of revenue to the states and localities under conditions of increasing prices. The major taxes at issue are state income and sales taxes and local property taxes. As of 1974, these were the major sources of revenue permitted by state constitutions to state and local governments, and they accounted for 61 percent of the revenues collected from their own sources. With the exception of the state income tax, these taxes did weigh most heavily on lower-income families. One calculation from an earlier period found property and sales taxes taking 17 percent of the incomes in the $4,000–$5,000 bracket, and only 4 percent of the incomes in the $10,000+ bracket.[16] Property and sales taxes—which account for 72 percent of state and local tax revenues—also have a more rigid rate structure than the income tax. As inflation raises the prices that state and local governments must pay for salaries, facilities, and supplies, the taxes on property and sales produce only moderate increases in revenue. It is true that inflation increases the value of real property and the magnitude of retail sales. Both features increase state and local collections from the property and sales taxes. However, these incre-ments are not as dramatic as those coming through a progressive income tax structure which boosts the rates applied to people as they move into higher tax brackets. Another problem is that state income taxes are not as steeply progressive as the Federal tax. Most state income taxes reach their highest rates for incomes of $15,000, while Federal rates keep increasing up to incomes of $100,000. The "flatness" of the state tax rates limits their revenue production during periods of rising incomes. Also, the income tax does not bulk as large in the revenues of state governments as it does in the revenues of the Federal government. In 1974 personal income taxes accounted for 16 percent of *state* collected revenues and 41 percent of *Federal* revenues. Because of their lower rates and lesser importance, income taxes do not provide the same boost to state revenues during inflation as they do to Federal revenues.

The constitutions of many states define their tax rates precisely. To make a change requires approval by the legislature and possibly by the voters in a statewide referendum. Given the general unpopularity of tax increases, these constitutional provisions present severe barriers to state and local finance. One detour around the tax problem is borrowing. The Federal government takes this route often to meet large bills for defense and major new domestic programs. But again due to provisions of most state constitutions, state and local government borrowing is restricted. Provisions either forbid indebtedness altogether, limit its magnitude to a small percentage of the currently available tax base, or restrict its use to a narrow range of governmental programs.

The revenue options that state constitutions permit to most local governments are even less generous than are permitted to the state. The typical constitution forces local governments to rely on the regressive and unpopular property tax, and it inhibits borrowing.

Other provisions of state constitutions are said to restrict govern-mental integration in urban areas. The typical metropolitan area is crossed with numerous jurisdictional lines that stand as barriers to coordinate social programs. There are separate municipal governments for the central city and the suburbs, plus special districts having responsibilities for education, libraries, parks, water, sanitation, or transportation. Officials in separate local jurisdictions cannot pursue coherent efforts throughout the urban area. There is a segregation of service demands and taxable resources on either side of these intra-urban boundaries. Some industrial and commercial areas surround themselves with municipal borders that create "tax islands" separated from citizens' needs for schools, parks, and police protection. It is clearly unfair for workers and customers to be denied any benefits from the tax payments of the industries or shopping centers that they support. Some upper-income suburbs use zoning or deed restrictions to keep out small home sites, and thus restrict the demands of low-income residents on their tax resources.

The urban governments with the greatest economic burdens are suburbs populated entirely by lower- or middle-income residents, sometimes with small scale and uniformly bleak neighborhoods. They are worse off than even the hard pressed central cities. Poor suburban communities typically face high demands for services without enough industry or commerce to spread the tax burden beyond the homeowner. The charge of "confiscatory" property taxes has its greatest merit when it is heard in residential communities that suffer from high rates and still cannot afford the services of their affluent neighbors.

How is it that state constitutions can prevent governmental integration in urban areas? By making it difficult to create broad-based, general-purpose local governments with responsibility for raising revenues, making policy, and providing service throughout the metropolis. Provisions in most state constitutions favor existing jurisdictions. Consolidations of different local governments depend on the formal consent of officials and citizens of each jurisdiction. At stake are the officials' jobs and status and the feelings of residents that their own communities are different from and independent of their neighbors.

The obvious remedy for fragmentation is to cut down on the number of counties, towns, villages, and special districts so that local government can obtain adequate geographical powers and revenue sources to manage local affairs effectively. The Committee for Economic Development, for example, would cut down the number of local governments from 81,000 to 16,000. But progress has been slow. The only really substantial reduction has been in school districts, from 67,000 in 1952 to 25,000 in 1966. Since 1900, the 3,000 counties have been reduced by a total of three.

> The towns, all 17,000 of them, continue to resist diminution. A
> town consolidation of Cattaragus County, New York, in 1965 was
> the first one in New York in 100 years.[17]

In most states it is easier to create new governments than to reduce the
surplus. Property owners in an unincorporated area can usually petition
their way to municipal status. This will protect them from annexation
by a nearby municipality and allow them to set their own tax, zoning,
and service policies. Such is the route of merchants or industrialists who
create tax islands for their business property and of homeowners who
screen out undesirables. Depending on the state, the newly formed
municipality may even qualify for state financial aids to help pay for its
minimal service requirements.

One product of surplus local governments is the abundance of local
officials. Many of these are elected out of an exaggerated faith in the
democratic process. Because of a long ballot for local elections, these
officials escape the careful scrutiny of the voters as well as of
professional superiors. Appointed local officers frequently earn their
job because of patronage rather than merit criteria. Most local
governments (as well as about half of the states) do not yet have a
comprehensive personnel system comparable to that of the United
States Civil Service Commission. Excess and inefficient employees not
only drain local resources and lack the technical proficiency to address
current social problems, but they stand as the most articulate and
organized spokespersons for the status quo.

> In all, some 500,000 elected and appointive officials govern local
> America. These county supervisors, highway commissioners, coro-
> ners, county clerks, prothonotaries, village trustees, town council-
> men, and even weed commissioners form a large, powerful, and
> ever vigilant cadre for the preservation of the status quo in general
> and their own offices in particular.[18]

SOME OTHER VIEWS OF THE STATES

There is some truth in these criticisms of state governments. There are
also counterarguments about the alleged defects of state constitutions.
Those provisions that inhibit the integration of local governments in
metropolitan areas, for example, seem less influential than the

widespread opposition to governmental integration that comes from the citizens themselves, from officers of local governments, and now from a new wave of scholarship that emphasizes the advantages of numerous local authorities.[19] Criticisms of state revenue provisions overlook enormous recent increases in the funds raised by state governments from their own citizens. State constitutions are also becoming more permissive in the revenue options allowed to state and local authorities. Increased funding has gone to aid local governments in the largest cities. And while the governors lack the kind of control over programs that is enjoyed by the President in the national government, many governors have led the successful drives to expand state tax programs and to use their funds to support progressive activities. There is much to praise in the states, as we shall see in later chapters. They offer accomplishments and opportunities, as well as shortcomings, for our consideration. This book's theme is that state governments should be our heroes and the subjects of our hopes instead of our whipping posts. In order to plan intelligently for the allocation of governmental responsibilities, we should know what the states have done and can do. The states' very existence provides some indication of vitality. Our Federal system is the oldest major government in the world. When the Constitution went into effect in 1789,

> the French monarchy still stood; there was a Holy Roman Emperor, a Venetian Republic and a Dutch Republic, an Autocrat in St. Petersburg, a Sultan-Caliph in Constantinople, an Emperor vested with the "mandate of Heaven" in Pekin and a Shogun ruling the hermit empire of Japan in the name of a secluded, impotent and almost unknown Mikado.[20]

The United States has avoided successful domestic rebellions. Despite occasional labor battles, draft riots, and self-destructive rampages in the black ghettos there has been only one Civil War. The establishment won and maintained its view of the Constitution. Despite the loss of that war by the side that voiced States' Rights, the victors preserved the states. Current interpretations of the Fourteenth Amendment (imposed on the South by the Federal Congress) make the states more humane and more responsive to their citizens than at any time in history. It is the *equal protection of the laws* clause of that amendment that enforces racial integration of public facilities and the one-man, one-vote apportionment of state legislatures. To be sure, the states themselves are not always responsible for their best moments. Some of what is good about them has come from Washington. However, many Federal programs started as the innovations of states.

The states show a capacity to handle some of the most controversial issues in society. State governments have shown the greatest capacity to raise taxes over the past two decades. During 1967, before the Federal courts took any decisive stand, 23 states considered changes in their abortion laws. Fourteen states dropped the death penalty for first-degree murder before the Federal courts addressed the issue. State regulatory commissions wrestled with utility rates and the siting of power plants with an eye to fuel conservation, health, safety, and aesthetics. With the onset of the oil embargo in 1973, states beat the national government to reduced speed limits. California pioneered in setting pollution-control standards for automobiles to be sold within that state and more recently has designed standards to require lower energy consumptions from refrigerators, freezers, and air conditioners. In both cases state officials did the groundwork of designing standards and administrative procedures in advance of the national government. The states administer numerous programs that operate so smoothly as to be prosaic. There seems little point in crediting the states with the effective control of sanitation in drinking water, milk, food markets, and restaurants. It is only after a trip to an exotic part of the world—or after the occasional failure in an American water system—that we think of state programs for licensing and inspection. The states also fail to get appropriate credit for the provision of higher education. Over 70 percent of college students take advantage of state institutions. According to one survey of graduate education, a state university (University of California at Berkeley) ranks most consistently as a top institution across a wide range of academic specialties—despite Ronald Reagan's incumbency.

THE SOURCES OF STATE VITALITY

What underpinnings of the state governments have kept them alive for so long? They receive support from a combination of constitutional provisions, laws, extralegal political institutions, custom, and attachment to the differences that have marked our regions since colonial times. The Constitution guarantees the states equal representation in the United States Senate, a state basis for selecting members of the United States House of Representatives, and state roles in the electoral college and the process of constitutional amendment. Some constitutional provisions make a direct grant of authority to the state governments, while others protect the states by assuring their citizens a role in making important decisions for the national government. The use of states as the electoral units for the House, Senate, and Presidency allow leading politicians in each state to exact promises from national candidates in exchange for their own campaign support. Insofar as the officials of leading cities have some influence over their state's political party (Chicago's late Mayor Richard Daley is the best example in recent years), this consultative role of state leaders in national politics also serves the interests of the cities.

Formal constitutional provisions merely set the stage for the protection of state and local interests within the Federal structure. A series of laws, customs, and political institutions provides the detailed bulwarks for state interests. The national government supported the activities of state and local governments with financial assistance totaling $53 billion in 1975. These programs are not simply imposed on the states. They are offered under terms that Congress defines as a result of consultations with the officials of state and local governments, and they are administered by procedures that are tolerable to most state officials and their friends in Congress.

Prominent, but extralegal, bulwarks of state governments are the political parties and "civil societies" that use state institutions to pursue or protect their goals. The American party system has state roots.[21] The 50 state parties are the key elements in national party structures. Members of the House and Senate and Presidential candidates owe political obligations to the leaders of state party organizations. Candidates' financial support comes from state party organizations. Presidential candidates gain their party nominations in state primaries and national conventions that are governed by the leaders of state parties. The national party offers few tangible incentives for state cooperation and holds no formal sanction over state recalcitrants. Some governors campaign openly in opposition to national party leaders, and some members of Congress compile voting records sharply at odds with their party's President. National Democrats have a problem with Southern conservatives who vote and campaign against their social, labor, and economic policies. In the fall of 1964 Barry Goldwater had to campaign against prominent state Republicans in New York, Illinois, and Michigan.

State populations show their loyalty to localities and regions in the face of outside pressure. This is most pronounced in the South, where state officials and private citizens responded in concert against Federal statutes and administrative "guidelines" that require racial integration. State officers and citizen groups in all regions seek Federal contracts for industries, Federal expenditures on military installations or public works, and national recognition of state historical celebrations and scenic attractions. These efforts involve chambers of commerce, elected officials of state and local governments, members of Congress, and individual business executives.

A feature that heightens the importance of the states in the Federal structure is the mixture of government responsibilities. There is no important domestic activity that is handled or financed solely by the Federal, state, or local governments. The fields that consume most domestic expenditures—education, highways, welfare, health, natural resources, public safety—are funded with a combination of Federal grants or loans and state and local taxes or service charges, and they are staffed partly by the personnel of national, state, and local governments. This means that national and local authorities must take account of state preferences in virtually all major policy decisions.

The remainder of this book leads the reader through several related inquiries. Chapter 2 deals with the economic, cultural, and political diversities that provided the original stimulus and the continuing justification for a Federal system of distinct state and national governments. Chapter 3 considers the financial resources of state governments; it is the key chapter for the thesis that state governments offer the strength necessary to maintain contemporary services. Chapter 3 also shows the financial burden carried by state governments and their record of meeting increasing demands with startling flexibility. Chapter 4 looks closely at state efforts in a policy area that receives prime time from politically aware citizens and should interest many readers of this book: higher education. State governments have moved strongly in a field that once was the province of private colleges. Not only did the states take over the field of higher education, but they did so in an era of expanding enrollments and increasingly sophisticated demands by students and faculty. Chapter 5 clarifies relationships between state capitals and Washington and inquires into the allegation that the national government is responsible for the good things done by the states. It shows that there is more myth than reality in the notion of "Federal control," and looks closely at three areas where there appears to be Federal dominance: transportation, welfare, and race. Even in these programs, state governments make commendable use of opportunities that exist within the framework of Federal efforts. Chapter 6 tackles the most persistent criticisms of state governments: the alleged failures in dealing with the urban crisis. To be sure, the states have not done enough for the cities. But neither have the national or local governments! Now, however, state governments are moving toward an urban orientation. And several basic features of national and local environments indicate that neither Washington nor City Hall will solve the urban crisis by itself. The cities need the states and are getting important help from them. Finally, a chapter on the future makes some modest predictions about the continuation of certain trends. It highlights state efforts in urban areas as the most likely field of growth, takes another look at the injustices done by those who malign state governments, and offers a proposal for modernizing Federal-state relations.

NOTES

1 The Federalist Papers, #46 (New York: Mentor Books, 1961, Clinton Rossiter, ed.).

2 John C. Calhoun, "The South Carolina Exposition," in Andrew M. Scott, ed., *Political Thought in America* (New York: Holt, 1960), pp. 236–243.

3 Terry Sanford, *Storm over the States* (New York: McGraw-Hill, 1967), p. 37.

4 Sanford, p. 21.

5 Martin Landau, "Baker v. Carr and the Ghost of Federalism," in Charles Cnudde and Deane E. Neubauer, eds., *Empirical Democratic Theory* (Chicago: Markham, 1969), p. 135.

6 Landau, p. 137.

7 Roscoe C. Martin, *The Cities and the Federal System* (New York: Atherton, 1965), pp. 45–47.

8 Martin, p. 78.

9   Martin, p. 78.

10 James L. Sundquist, *Making Federalism Work* (Washington: Brookings, 1969), pp. 265–266.

11 Sanford, p. 1. See also Dan W. Lufkin, *Many Sovereign States: A Case for Strengthening State Government—An Insider's Account* (New York: McKay, 1975).

12 M. Kent Jennings and Harmon Zeigler, "The Salience of American State Politics," *American Political Science Review,* 64 (June 1970), 523–535.

13 Sundquist, p. 271.

14 Henry S. Reuss, *Revenue-Sharing: Crutch or Catalyst for State and Local Governments?* (New York: Praeger, 1970), pp. 71–73.

15 Thomas J. Anton, *The Politics of State Expenditure in Illinois* (Urbana: University of Illinois Press, 1966), p. 146.

16 Reuss, p. 27.

17 Reuss, p. 44.

18 Reuss, p. 46.

19 See, for example, Vincent Ostrom, *The Intellectual Crisis in American Public Administration* (University: University of Alabama Press, 1974), especially chap. V.

20 D. W. Brogan, *Politics in America* (New York: Harper, 1954), p. 18.

21 Morton Grodzins, "American Political Parties and the American System," *Western Political Quarterly,* 13 (December 1960), pp. 974–998; and Daniel J. Elazar, *American Federalism: A View from the States* (New York: Thomas Y. Crowell).

Chapter 2

A Justification for Strong State Governments: Diversity in Culture, Economics, and Politics

The prominent figures in the recent years of state politics range in ideology and style from Nelson Rockefeller and Jerry Brown to Ronald Reagan, Lester Maddox, and George Wallace. This is not a new situation. The history of state politics features Huey Long, Robert LaFollette, and Soapy Williams. During their terms, each typified his state and set it on paths that are still evident. Distinctiveness and diversity have always marked the American states. Because of sharp differences among the British Colonies, the founding fathers created a Federal system instead of a unitary state. Diversity remains and begs to be examined by those who would understand American politics.

The focus of this chapter is diversity in state cultures, economics, and politics. This diversity frustrates many observers who insist on government that is uniformly and immediately progressive. Other observers ignore the bright spots amid the diversity, and remain preoccupied with the dark sides of the backward states. Friends of the states should find both hope and amusement in the diversity: hope from the innovative character of many state programs and the progress that all states have shown in recent years and from the opportunities for diverse lifestyles that appear in the states, plus at least some amusement in the idiosyncracies and anomalies that remain in state politics.

We pursue the topic of state diversity in several ways: by reciting some oddities and ironies of individual states; by examining regional patterns of state politics, economics, culture, and policies; by highlighting cases of progressive social policies that appear in some states despite economic and cultural conditions that seem to dictate a lack of such activities; and by conceding the problems that exist because of state diversity.

In some respects, the diversity of state cultures, economics, and politics is simply interesting. It enlivens public affairs in what otherwise might be an unvarying mass society of 215 million. In other respects, diversity shows the opportunities for creative policy making, insofar as no state's social, economic, or political conditions are so powerful as influences on its policies as to discourage the bold innovator. In any case, diversity is a fact of life that we seem destined to have for its bads as well as its goods. State differences go back to the beginning of this country, and account for basic features of our society and government. These differences do produce some problems in unequal citizen opportunities from one state to another, and in interstate coordination of complex programs. For the solution of many such problems, however, we must look to the unique powers of the national government and not simply curse the states for their origin.

Flamboyance is one trait that unites Rockefeller, Reagan, Maddox, and Wallace. If we look beneath their first layer of public reputation, we find another trait they hold in common: a complexity in their personal records that reflects the complexity of their states. As Governor of California, Reagan was the chief bogeyman in the demonology of liberals. Yet there are undoubtedly some middle-of-the-road and even left-of-center Californians who voted him back to office in 1970 with a majority of 54 percent, while they voted out the Conservative Superintendent of Public Instruction Max Rafferty and Conservative United States Senator George Murphy. Even Maddox and Wallace are more complex than their first impression. As Governor of Georgia, Lester Maddox was as much a populist as a racist, as witnessed by some leading blacks in state politics.[1] Yet Maddox continued to insist that he was all for segregation and against socialism. Wallace cannot shake a racist label despite efforts in that direction during his Presidential campaigns of 1968, 1972, and 1976. To his credit, it must be said that his first term as Governor brought Alabama several new institutions of higher education and many miles of new highway. The improvements provide economic opportunities to blacks as well as whites. Rockefeller's complexity is of a different order. He is the Republican who continued New York's leadership in several fields of public service and elevated a fledgling system of higher education to the most comprehensive—and certainly the most expensive—east of Ohio. He won a fourth consecutive term in 1970 but could not hold together his own political party. Spiro Agnew identified Rockefeller's appointee to the United States Senate as the most obnoxious of the Capitol's Republicans and helped elect Conservative James Buckley in his place.

For the observer who is sensitive to regional patterns, Massachusetts means political clambakes; Italian, Irish, and Yankee names balancing one another on the state ballot; intense Catholic versus Protestant feelings about public schools and birth control; and frequent exposés of public corruption. Georgia's politicians make their public appeals with barbecue and sweetened iced tea or Coca-Cola; their names are as uniformly Anglo-Saxon as the characters in *Dick and Jane;* and their campaigns center on roads, schoolteachers' salaries, the assorted economic woes of the little man, and the eternal verities of Old and New Testaments. While Georgia's politicians abstain in public, Wisconsin's slosh beer with the voters. German bratwurst takes the place of barbecue or clambake. Issues and sometimes sophisticated ideology dominate Wisconsin's campaign, taking the place of the scandals that appear in other states. Wisconsin elections deal with dairy farming and whatever else troubles serious people in the country: war, crime, or rebellious youth. A vestigial tax on oleomargarine and a low tax on beer are as typical of Wisconsin politics as the ubiquitous peanut sellers who prowl the Georgia capitol when the legislature is in session and the job-seekers and arrangers who hang on at the State House in Boston.

Eighteenth-century diversity prompted the construction of a Federal system in the fledgling United States, and twentieth-century diversity helps explain the vitality of federalism. The original diversity was a product of distinct colonial settlements. The recruiters for the colonies of Plymouth, Massachusetts Bay, New York, Pennsylvania, Virginia, Maryland, and Georgia sought out different kinds of settlers from England and the Continent. By the time of Independence internal migration had blurred the initial patterns, but other diversities were established by the heavy use of slave labor in the Southern colonies and by the development of distinctive political styles among such Northern colonies as Massachusetts, Rhode Island, and Pennsylvania. Today the North-South demarcation remains the most distinctive internal border between different cultures, economic conditions, political styles, and modes of public policy. These differences take advantage of state governments to reinforce their hold on public affairs. An important justification for the federal nature of American government rests upon these internal differences.

Distance had a lot to do with the establishment of a Federal system. The distance between North and South in an era of primitive means of transportation and communication helps explain the roles assigned to the states in the revolutionary government and in the later Constitution. Any effort at a strong central government would have been more ambitious than wise. The combined features of distance and diversity also prompted the establishment of Federal arrangements elsewhere in the world. Canada and the Soviet Union have internal cultural diversity and great distances. Switzerland has more diversity than distance. However, its geographical difficulties imposed severe problems of communication and transportation across only short distances, especially during the thirteenth century when the Swiss federal structure developed. Australia's federal system rests more on distance between its centers of population than cultural diversity.

NORTHEAST, SOUTH, WEST, AND MIDDLE WEST

Diversity appears to be more important than distance as a continuing explanation for American Federalism. There is no longer any problem of transportation or communication to explain the political vitality of distinct state governments. State boundaries that go back in time and almost never change give people geopolitical reference points. That sharp political differences remain among states and regions is evident to all who would look. Although gross regional differences are most well known, the major regions are not uniform within themselves. There are some sharp differences from one neighbor to another.[2]

The Northeast

Even in tiny New England there are dissimilarities among states in the north and south sections. All New England shares the common characteristics of early settlement, a common ethnic-religious background, state constitutions that are relatively old, brief, and simple, a tendency to administer locally many programs that in other regions are handled by state agencies, large state legislatures that typically include at least one representative from each town, and the primacy of the town meeting in rural areas. Yet Maine, New Hampshire, and Vermont remain relatively rural, Yankee, Protestant, and Republican. In Massachusetts, Rhode Island, and Connecticut the Democratic descendants of Catholic immigrants from Ireland, French Canada, plus Southern and Eastern Europe have replaced the Yankees. New England politicians identify candidates in ethnic terms and seek to balance party tickets with a proper representative of each group. Certain places on the ticket are considered the legitimate possession of an ethnic group. For many years the Democratic nominee for Connecticut's at-large congressional seat was a Pole, and one Portuguese after another succeeded to the office of Registar of Voters in Fall River, Massachusetts. The ethnic fixation of New England politicians is as prominent as the racial fixation of Southern politicians. In both regions there is a tendency to make electoral appeals based not on policy issues but on one's emotional identification with one's grandfather's culture.

Not only ethnicity, but the related Catholic-Protestant division affects politics in the Northeast. Birth control legislation imposed on Massachusetts and Connecticut by Victorian Protestants in the nineteenth century has recently provoked antagonism between Catholics (who support the anti-birth control legislation) and Protestants, Jews, and other non-Catholics who oppose. Many schoolchildren in the Northeast attend Catholic parochial schools, and public support of parochial education is another source of political friction. In Rhode Island, New Hampshire, Pennsylvania, New York, Massachusetts, and New Jersey, over 20 percent of the elementary and secondary pupils attend non-public schools. While Catholic leaders argue that public school funds should supplement the private support given to parochial

schools, non-Catholics complain that parochial school enrollments serve
to lessen the support given to public school budgets.

The Northeast is the most congested and industrialized region.
Many political alignments and disputes draw their energy from the
region's economy. More than elsewhere in the United States, Democrats
represent the workers and speak out for generous social programs, while
Republicans represent bankers, business management, and small town
merchants. Yet historic patterns blur as the children of ethnic
Democrats move to the suburbs and encounter Republican temptations.
No longer are the region's Republicans universally committed to high
tariffs and low taxes. The New York Republican party shows its inner
tensions most clearly, with Governor Rockefeller and Senator Javits
boycotting Barry Goldwater's 1964 campaign and Senator Goodell
being singled out by Spiro Agnew in 1970 and replaced by another
Republican (actually labeled Conservative), James Buckley.

When tensions occur within the national Republican party, they
frequently see politicians from the Northeast against those from the
rest of the country. Edward Brooke (Mass.), Clifford Case (N.J.), Hugh
Scott (Pa.), and Jacob Javits (N.Y.) have voted like good Democrats in
the United States Senate. The blue-collar nature of so many of their
constituents, the Democratic loyalties of the region's ethnic groups, and
a *noblesse-oblige* tradition among the region's upper class have kept any
ambitious Republican from accepting too many GOP traditions.

The South

Although the South appears distinct as a cultural and political region,
there are varying definitions of its geographical outline. Some denote
the South simply as those states that seceded from the Union to form
the Confederacy: Virginia, North Carolina, South Carolina, Tennessee,
Georgia, Alabama, Florida, Mississippi, Arkansas, Louisiana, and Texas.
Others combine this region with some or all of the Border states—
Delaware, Maryland, West Virginia, Kentucky, Missouri, and Oklahoma—which are akin to the South because they received much of their
initial population from there, attempted to secede from the Union (the
stars of Kentucky and Missouri are included in the Confederacy's flag),
or legislated statewide racial segregation of public education.

There are significant economic, social, and political differences
among such "Southern" states as Delaware, West Virginia, Arkansas,

Florida, Mississippi, and Texas. But each state of the South shows some of the following characteristics: widespread poverty; low levels of popular education; a large population of nonwhites who have felt the cultural and political disadvantages of slavery and segregation; low levels of participation in politics (by both whites and nonwhites); widespread conservatism, both social and political; one-party politics; governors who have strong political clout; and a powerful role for the states in dealing with their local governments.

The economic and cultural poverty of the South reveals itself in low levels of personal income per capita, low levels of adult education, high illiteracy, and a high incidence of armed service inductees who fail the mental examination. Few Southern colleges attain national academic recognition.

One-party domination of state and local politics in the South means that factions of the Democratic party do battle with each other. In some states these factions gain a permanence not unlike that of organized parties: Long and anti-Long factions in Louisiana have taken party-like positions against one another for many years. In other Southern states, factions are more temporary in their identification with individual politicians. A disadvantage of factional politics is the lack of predictability. In the absence of permanently organized political parties whose positions in any one year resemble those taken in earlier years, voters are hard pressed to identify their votes for one candidate or another with the services they will likely receive after the election. And the elected legislator lacks the cues that policy-relevant parties might provide to help on a piece of legislation. Partly because of the absence of a well-organized partisan opposition, Southern governors attain considerable political strength. The Southern governor is almost solely in control of the resources that can attract support from legislators: government jobs, roads, improvements in the state institutions within a legislator's district, and government purchasing.[3]

The Southern governor profits from the historic centralization of government in his region. The colonial South differed from the North in lacking a population sufficient to develop numerous small towns and in lacking the religious inclination of New England Congregationalists to nurture autonomous local units. Because of the poverty among present-day citizens, many of the South's city and county governments do not have sufficient economic resources within their jurisdiction to

support public services. This adds to the importance of state governments in the South. The tax on real property that is constitutionally
available to local governments does not work in poverty. With
depression, the value of real property is low, as is the capacity of
individual property owners to pay large sums of money to the
government. In contrast, the state-collected sales tax remains productive in a depressed situation as people continue to make retail purchases
in at least small amounts; likewise, state income taxes take revenue in
tolerably small amounts as workers receive their wages. Moreover, state
taxes have access to the economy of their entire jurisdiction and can
draw wealth from wealthy urban and suburban areas in order to help
support programs in poor rural counties. Because Southern states are
inclined by history and economics to pay for and provide services that
local governments provide elsewhere, Southern governors and other
state officials have a great deal to say about the salary of schoolteachers, the location of new or improved roads, and public medical
facilities.

The West

Like other regions, the West is defined in various ways. Although a
common demarcation begins at the eastern borders of Montana,
Wyoming, Colorado, and New Mexico, some notions of the West
include states on the Mississippi River. Within this larger region, the
Plains states, Rocky Mountain states, and the Pacific Coastal states are
distinct subregions.

Much of the politics that is typically Western results from
topographic or economic peculiarities such as population diffusion,
huge empty spaces, uneven land surface, mineral resources, and uneven
distribution of water. Out of these features comes a pervasive concern
for transportation and resource development. Another feature of
Western politics is a high incidence of land ownership by the Federal
government. There is no state east of the Rocky Mountains where the
Federal government owns *more* than 13 percent of the land and no
state west of this line where it owns *less* than 29 percent. Several
Western states approach Nevada's Federal land ownership of 86
percent. Although much Federal land has limited economic potential,
its ownership is a source of contention. Members of Congress have
established the principle that Federal ownership (even of marginal

lands) carries Federal responsibility for economic assistance. Western states score highest in their proportionate use of Federal money. Eleven states west of the Rockies average 34 percent greater Federal aid per capita than thirty-seven Eastern and Middle Western states. If Alaska and Hawaii are included in the Western group, its proportionate advantage increases further. This Western bonanza shows what equal representation in the Senate can do for small population states with a sense of affinity.[4]

Western politics shows the highest levels of voter turnout and the closest contests between Democrats and Republicans of any region. The intense party competition reflects the later settlement of the West. The greatest intranational migration occurred after the Civil War and settled the West with both Republican Northerners and Democratic Southerners. Since that time no trauma approaching the magnitude of the Civil War has aligned Westerners generally into one party or another. As in other parts of the country, the early generations passed on their partisan loyalties. In the West, this has meant a continuation of close elections until the present. Along with its competition, the West has weak party organizations. This is noticed in the use of electoral devices that strengthen the voter at the expense of the party: referendum and recall provisions; Washington's "blanket primary" that permits a voter to select candidates in both parties at the same time; the now-repealed California statute that allowed a candidate to file in the primary of both parties; and the extraparty "Democratic clubs" of California. The West exhibits weak party organizations along with strong party competition, whereas the South demonstrates weak party organizations in the presence of little party competition. At least in these cases, regional peculiarities appear to be more important than general principles of party organization and competition.

Some traits of the West divide its subregions against one another. While all the Western states have a strong interest in water resource development, they oppose one another in the selection of sites for development and the formulas for water distribution. Nevada and California, for example, align themselves against Arizona for use of the Colorado River flow. And while the coastal states of Washington and California reap great economic benefits from defense contracts, other Western states urge Federal agencies to distribute government contracts on the basis of economic needs.

The Middle West

The Middle West is the region left over after the remaining states are assigned to the Northeast, South, or West. In northern areas of the Middle West the countryside offers rich farmland and Republican loyalties. The cities are industrial and Democratic. In southern areas of the Middle West, however, Democratic inclinations appear in rural areas. These patterns reflect the origin of early agricultural settlements: those in the north were populated from antislavery Northeastern states or by German or Scandinavian immigrants, and those of the south were settled by secession-inclined elements from Maryland, Virginia, the Carolinas, Kentucky, and Tennessee. In Ohio, Indiana, and Illinois, Northern settlers came overland and settled in the upper counties, while Southerners came down the Ohio River and settled from the bottom upward. During the Civil War these two population groups produced explosive cleavages within the Middle West. By now, their settlements and ideologies have become mixed throughout Ohio, Indiana, and Illinois, but their disparate origins continue to affect state policies. Each of these states offers liberal urban Democrats and some rural Republicans steeped in a progressive tradition, plus rural conservatives who are both Democrats and Republicans. Each party in Ohio, Indiana, and Illinois provides an ideological home for present-day liberals or conservatives. Partly because of the lack of sharp policy differences between parties, the interparty competition revolves about patronage jobs, personalities, and state contracts, rather than issues of current policy.[5]

REGIONAL TRAITS IN THE 1970s

The U.S. Bureau of the Census provides a continuing picture of regional differences in population and economic traits. By comparing some of the very latest reports with those earlier in the century, we can see which regions are growing most rapidly, and which are stable or suffering decline. Table 2-1 reports two of the most widely used indicators of regional differences—population and per capita personal income. One charts the movements of people from one region to another, and the other measures the relative well-being of people in each region.

Table 2-1   Regional Traits in Income and Population, 1929-1974

	Per capita income*				Percentage change		Population (× 1,000,000)				Percentage change	
	1929	1960	1970	1974	1929-1974	1960-1974	1910	1960	1970	1974	1910-1974	1960-1974
United States	$703	$2,222	$3,966	$5,434	673	145	92.2	179.3	200.3	211.4	129	18
New England	876	2,430	4,304	5,697	550	134	6.6	10.5	11.7	12.2	85	16
Mid-Atlantic	979	2,582	4,475	6,033	516	134	19.3	34.2	36.7	37.3	93	9
East North Central	803	2,391	4,130	5,733	614	140	18.3	36.2	39.8	40.8	123	3
West North Central	572	2,061	3,749	5,203	810	152	11.6	15.3	16.2	16.7	44	3
South Atlantic	462	1,843	3,618	5,073	998	175	12.2	26.0	30.1	33.2	172	28
East South Central	348	1,497	2,990	4,279	1,130	186	8.4	12.1	12.5	13.4	60	7
West South Central	436	1,819	3,406	4,622	960	154	8.8	17.0	18.9	20.6	134	21
Mountain	580	2,087	3,601	4,965	756	138	2.6	6.9	8.2	9.4	261	36
Pacific	911	2,612	4,383	5,903	548	126	4.4	21.2	26.2	27.8	532	31

Sources: U.S. Bureau of the Census, *Statistical Abstract of the United States, 1961, 1975* (Washington: GPO, 1962, 1975); and *World Almanac, 1977* (New York: Newspaper Enterprises Association, 1976).
*Not available prior to 1929.

As of 1974, the Southern regions remained in their expected place at the bottom of the economic scale. The greatest wealth appeared on the West Coast and in the Northeast. The East South Central region (Alabama, Mississippi, Kentucky, and Tennessee) is the poorest. Its per capita income is only $4,279. The wealthiest are Mid-Atlantic and Pacific, both with per capita incomes above $5,900. The image of the South changes, however, when viewed over time. Southern regions show the greatest increases of per capita income over 1929–1974 and during the most recent 14 years. In the same periods, the wealthier regions have grown the least. Thus, the extremes of wealth and poverty appear to be closing as the poorest regions are catching up with the rest of the country. In 1929 the wealthiest region had a per capita income that was 2.8 times that of the poorest region, but the gap was only 1.4 times in 1974.

Increases in population favor both Western and Southern regions. Florida is the fastest growing state in the South; it increased its population by 79 percent between 1950 and 1960 and then by 63 percent between 1960 and 1974. In the West, Nevada is growing even faster: by 78 percent and then by another 97 percent in the 1950s and from 1960 to 1974. In 1960 Nevada competed with Alaska for the bottom ranking in population; now it has climbed above Delaware, Vermont, and Wyoming and will probably overtake North Dakota, South Dakota, and Montana before 1980.

NATIONALIZATION AND THE FUTURE
OF REGIONAL DIVERSITY

What about the claim that the country is becoming increasingly uniform? Are the distinctive patterns of states and regions succumbing to more dominant national influences? Do the numerous programs of the Federal government and their controls over recipients obliterate distinctive state programs?

The "nationalization" of American politics is said to be an aspect of larger developments that are producing an integrated national economy and culture. Several changes may reflect a growing nationalism at the same time that they further its development: the prominence of network programming on television; the absorption of locally owned newspapers into national chains; the assimilation of local industries by national corporations; the growing homogeneity of working conditions and consumer goods across the country; the development of national "labor markets" for many professions and skilled trades; the movement of people across state and regional boundaries, most often from the north and east to the south and west; and the increasing number of state and local government programs that receive funds and performance standards from Federal agencies.

The nationalization of American politics is a matter of some dispute among political scientists.[6] There is less dispute about the reality of nationalization than about its extent. The various regions are more alike in their cultures, economics, and politics than in the not-too-distant past. Yet the process of nationalization has not proceeded so far as to obliterate the regions. Those who perceive homogenization may exaggerate the speed, if not the direction, of political change. The influence of regional historical experiences and the continuing inclination of state and community leaders to acquire their policy norms from neighboring states may be powerful enough to resist the often-cited pressures for nationalizing.

An examination of one reputed nationalizing force—Federal grants-in-aid—reveals that it actually contains opportunities for the further development of regional differences. As we see in Chapter 5, state and local governments do not act as underlings who respond obediently to the temptations of Washington gold. State officials and political leaders present their demands for increased aid to the Federal Congress and help write the performance standards that will govern program administration. Spokespersons for the states recognize the opportunities presented by the checks and balances of the national government. They use alliances with congressional committees to obtain concessions from agencies or else use an alliance with an administrative agency to win concessions from a congressional committee. Federal programs usually permit state agencies to provide services not previously supported with state funds. Moreover, the states share certain decisions in these new programs with Federal administrators. If *power* is defined as the ability to control one's environment, then increased knowledge, technological ability, and economic resources permit Federal *and* state governments to increase their power simultaneously. In their exercise of new discretions, state officials are guided not only by national norms, but also in large measure by the norms that regional administrators have evolved out of the cultural environment and interstate contacts guiding many of their decisions. The result may be the evolution of new regional standards relevant to the Federal programs. Twenty-five years after Federally aided welfare programs began, the payments made by Southern states were considerably lower than in other regions and lower even than the Southern economy leads us to expect.[7] State officials in the South tailor their Federally aided welfare activities to the conservative antiwelfare views that prevail in that region.

It is true that economics and politics in each of the regions are becoming, in certain respects, more like those of other regions. Generally speaking, all states are showing an increase in economic and political "development"—measured as personal income, urbanism, industrialization, plus popular participation in politics and financial support for public services. The "underdeveloped" states are showing more progress than the "developed" ones, so that ranges between extreme regions are becoming smaller and all states are clustering more tightly around the national averages. Yet this nationalization is not occurring uniformly: in some cases individual regions are not sharing in the general progress toward national patterns, and the states in each region are becoming even more like their neighbors than like states in distant regions. Regional homogeneity grows along with national homogeneity.[8]

One claim of those who see American politics becoming nationalized is that residents of different regions are thinking more alike than in the recent past. It is difficult to demonstrate this tendency with certainty. What is clear, however, is that Southerners on the average continue to think differently than other Americans. Gallup polls find Southerners tending to be more conservative in matters of race, personal lifestyle, and domestic politics, and more willing to accept the use of war in international affairs. Table 2-2 shows some representative responses.

The evidence is mixed with respect to the nationalization of state politics. The South remains distinctive in numerous traits even while it has moved toward national patterns elsewhere. It is no longer solidly Democratic in Presidential elections. It favored Republican over Democratic candidates in 1952, 1956, 1968, and 1972. In 1964, the region as a whole voted Democratic but gave more support to Barry Goldwater than he received anywhere but in his native Arizona. On the

Table 2-2   Selected Items Showing Regional Differences in Public Opinion

Question	U.S., %	South, %
College students' placement of their political views according to the following choices:		
Far left or left	37	27
Middle of the road	41	52
Right or far right	17	19
Male college students asked about their preferred hair length:		
Short, traditional length	45	50
Long, but not over ears	23	23
Over ears, but not to shoulder	20	14
To or below shoulder	7	8
Afro	4	4
General population asked their opinion of current level of defense spending:		
Too little	11	17
Too much	50	37
About right	31	36
General population asked if they would be more or less likely to vote for their favored Presidential candidate if he or she selected a black Vice Presidential running mate:		
More likely	13	5
Less likely	24	42
No difference	57	48

Source: The Gallup Poll: Public Opinion 1935-1971, volume 3 (New York: Random House, 1972), pp. 2287, 2290, 2298, 2327. All the above items were surveyed in 1971.

state level, however, the South remains almost solid Democratic. In 1975 88 percent of state legislative seats in the former Confederacy were Democratic compared with 62 percent elsewhere. The region's delegations in Congress were 74 percent Democratic, while those of other regions were 63 percent Democratic. Overall political participation has increased in the South along with increased black activity, but the region's citizens remain less active than those elsewhere. The

South's voting rate was 11 percent below the national average in the elections of 1972 and 1974.

Southern states have narrowed the spending gap between themselves and the national averages since 1903, but the movement is not simply a product of the recent past. State government expenditures in the eleven states of the Confederacy reached a level that was 76 percent of the national average as early as 1929, but the region's progress was set back during the Depression. In an early war year (1942) the spending of Southern states returned to 73 percent of the national average and then spurted to 81 percent by 1947. By 1974, state expenditures in the region had moved little (relative to the national average) beyond their level of 1947—to only 88 percent of the national average.

The lack of steady progress in expenditures of Southern states may reflect the holding power of regional norms despite considerable economic development. During 1952-1974, per capita personal income in the old Confederacy went from 68 percent of the national average to 83 percent of the national average. Meanwhile, state expenditures per capita moved only slightly: from 87 to 88 percent of the national average.

SOURCES OF REGIONAL PECULIARITY

What are the origins of persistent differences among the regions? Some of the most distinctive traits were brought to this country in earlier forms by European immigrants and then distributed throughout the United States by subsequent generations. Across the Northern states and into the Plains region there are traces of Puritan ethics that came to Massachusetts in the seventeenth century. Across the Southern states from the tidewater to Arizona, there went attitudes about traditional elites and the proper status of slaves and (later) free blacks that left their mark on Jim Crow statutes.[11] The original settlers of the middle colonies were diverse in their backgrounds, but seemed to resemble one another in a striving to get ahead. One student of American cultural patterns writes about the middle colonies:

> Groups of quite different ethnic and religious backgrounds, primarily from England and the interior Germanic states, settled the middle parts of the nation, beginning with the Middle Atlantic

states of New York, New Jersey, Pennsylvania, Delaware, and Maryland. The majority of these highly diverse groups, which together established the basic patterns of American pluralism, were united by one common bond in particular—the search for individual opportunity in the New World. Unlike the Puritans who sought communal as well as individualistic goals in their migrations, the pursuit of private ends predominated among the settlers of the middle states. Though efforts were made to establish morally purposeful communities, particularly in Pennsylvania, the very purpose of these communities was to develop pluralistic societies dedicated to individual freedom to pursue private goals, to the point of making religion a private matter, an unheard-of step at the time. The political culture of the middle states reflected this distinctive emphasis on private pursuits from the first and, by the end of the colonial period, a whole system of politics designed to accommodate itself to such a culture had been developed . . .

These groups also moved westward across Pennsylvania into the central parts of Ohio, Indiana, and Illinois, then on into Missouri. There, reinforced by immigrants from western Europe and the lower Germanic states who shared the same attitudes, they developed extensions of their pluralistic patterns.[12]

Some backwaters attracted peculiar migrants and retain much of their primitive character today. In his incisive and sympathetic book about eastern Kentucky, Harry M. Caudill traces its contemporary poverty to the background of the first settlers. They were not yeomen familiar with the soil but the very lowest class from England's urban slums. In Virginia they escaped—or worked their way out of—indenture and learned the rudiments of farming from the Indians. The agriculture they learned was slash—burn—and deplete, with little concern for replenishing the land. Two centuries later the mineowners found the settlers willing partners in their efforts to deplete the earth. Payments for mineral rights and miners' wages were not invested in the future of oneself or one's children, but spent on the most attractive available consumer goods. When the mineowners opposed fair taxation for the support of public services, the miners agreed. Even today the counties of eastern Kentucky present some of the last areas where votes are bought and paid for on election day and where even the public schools are staffed by hacks of the local political organization.[13]

No explanation of contemporary state politics is complete without reference to the sharing of major historical trauma by regional neighbors. Much of the contemporary South reflects the accretions built up in response to slavery, war, Reconstruction, and continued poverty plus racial segregation. Policies from Wisconsin through the Dakotas are left over from agricultural depression, railroad troubles, and populist-progressive victories after the turn of the century. Rocky Mountain states have more generous social policies than expected on the basis of their current economic traits—due to earlier reactions against the free enterprise excesses of their lumber and mineral barons.

REGIONALISM AMONG GOVERNMENT OFFICIALS

The work habits of contemporary state officials reinforce other factors producing likenesses in the politics of neighboring states.[14] Regional consultation is a common practice among state administrators. Agency personnel in Florida, Georgia, Kentucky, and Mississippi were asked to identify the states they had contacted for program-related information. The 67 officers made 198 nominations of such states. Eighty-seven percent of their nominations were in the region composed of the eleven states of the Confederacy and the Border states of Delaware, Maryland, Kentucky, West Virginia, and Oklahoma. Thirty-five percent of the states nominated bordered directly on those of the respondents. It is conceivable that Southerners are more parochial in their perceptions of reference-states than officials in other sections of the country; yet officials elsewhere typically refer to states that are immediate or near neighbors when they are asked to name their reference groups.

Which states in each region are usually the subject of emulation by their neighbors? The comments of several officials suggest that states which have acquired a reputation for leadership in a certain field of service are sought out disproportionately for their advice. Professor Jack L. Walker of the University of Michigan gathered evidence on the timing of innovations in 48 states. He has ranked the states according to their tendency to adopt programs earlier than other states. New York and Massachusetts play leadership roles in the Northeast; Michigan and Wisconsin in the middle section of the country; California on the West Coast; Colorado in the Mountain region; and Louisiana and Virginia in the South.[15] Officials of leading states within each region are likely to generate their own innovations or take their cues from leaders in other regions. The follow-the-regional-leader communications network that prevails among most states helps to isolate their officials from direct national influences and permits the development of regional approaches to new programs—even when such programs are sponsored and "regulated" by Federal agencies.

The tendency of political leaders and government officials to acquire their cues from regional neighbors has several causes: the belief that neighbors have problems similar to one's own; the attitude among officials and interested citizens that it is "legitimate" to adapt one's programs to those of nearby governments; and the nature of organizational affiliations that put officers into frequent contact with counterparts in neighboring governments.

The belief that officials of neighboring jurisdictions have similar problems means several things. Partly it means that elites in neighboring states have encountered policy questions similar to those currently being faced; consequently the neighbor is likely to have a concrete suggestion to offer or to be informed about the pitfalls to be encountered along the way to certain solutions. Partly, too, it means that the neighboring government is serving a population akin to one's own, with similar needs for public service and similar demands on government agencies. The neighboring government's economy is likely to be similar, presenting a comparable set of resources and needs to government agencies. The same resemblance usually exists between the political environments, with respect to the levels of service that can receive the support of citizen groups and state officials. Regionally oriented public officials have a sense of interstate competition that inclines them to services no lower and taxes no higher than regional norms.

STATE ECONOMICS, CULTURE, POLITICS, AND PUBLIC POLICY

Not all of the diversity among the states follows regional patterns. There are numerous cases of individual states that do not "fit" their regional patterns in certain features of political activity. Many state activities follow economic patterns; wealthy and poor states act distinctively no matter where their regional location.[16] Citizens of well-to-do states tend to be active in politics, and the parties of these states compete actively against one another. State and local policies tend to be generous, especially in the fields of education, health, and public welfare. Most interesting are the cases that do not fit any pattern. Individual states go off on tangents that are not easily explained by regional history or current economics. Some offer commendable public services despite environments that seem hostile.

Economic conditions do not explain the high scores on political participation and party competition in the mountain states of Montana, Idaho, Wyoming, and Utah. These states fall below the national averages on income, industrialization, and urbanism, but in contrast to the general economic pattern show the highest scores in the country for voter turnout and party competition. At the other end of the political scale, the low scores or turnout and competition in the South are not explained by economic conditions. It is true that the Southern states are the poorest in the country, but their rates of participation and competition are even lower than expected on the basis of their economic traits.[17] Texas and Florida are wealthier than their neighbors, but except for certain prominent statewide contests, their politics remain Democratic and their voter turnout is below the national average. In many sections of those states no Republican has a ghost of a chance in running for a seat in the state legislature or a place on a county commission.

Political cultures differ from one state and region to the next and leave their imprint on public affairs. Professor Daniel J. Elazar finds evidence of "Moralist," "Individualist," and "Traditionalist" cultures that appear in different degrees of strength and in various combinations with each other across the country.[18] The traditional culture is concentrated most heavily in the South, although it is diluted by moralist cultures in the mountain counties of the Appalachians and Ozarks. Moralist cultures are most apparent in the Upper Middle West and (a geographic exception) Oregon. Individualism is a secondary trait throughout much of the country, but figures most strongly in the Western states of Nevada and Wyoming. Figure 2-1 shows how Elazar locates each of the three cultures.

As Elazar describes them, a Moralist orientation considers participation to be the duty of all citizens, who should involve themselves in politics for the sake of the commonwealth; an Individualist culture holds that participation is something to be engaged in more narrowly for the sake of improving one's own position; and the Traditionalist culture reserves participation for those with elite status. In its

Figure 2-1 The regional distribution of political cultures within the states.

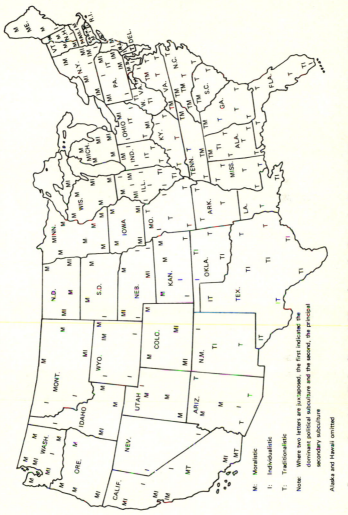

M: Moralistic

I: Individualistic

T: Traditionalistic

Note: Where two letters are juxtaposed, the first indicated the dominant political subculture and the second, the principal secondary subculture

Alaska and Hawaii omitted

Source: *American Federalism: A View from the States* by Daniel J. Elazar, copyright © 1966 by Thomas Y. Crowell Company, Inc. with permission of the publisher.

39

orientation toward bureaucracy, the Moralist culture values extensive, well-paid, and professional administrative corps at all levels of government; the Individualist culture views bureaucracy as a potential fetter to private affairs, but also as a resource that public officials can use to further their own goals; and the Traditionalist culture opposes the growth of bureaucracy as a restraint on the political elite. The cultures also differ in their views toward the government's intervention in the community. The Moralist welcomes intervention for the good of the commonwealth; the Individualist would minimize intervention to permit a balance of satisfactions from activities in the private and the public sector; and the Traditionalist would oppose all government interventions except those necessary to maintain the existing power structure. Or a related dimension, the Moralist culture welcomes the initiation of new programs for the good of the community; in the Individualist culture, new programs would be initiated only if they could be described as political favors that would elicit favors in return for those who provided the programs; and the Traditionalist would accept new programs only if they were necessary for the maintenance of the status quo.

Professor Elazar's designations of political culture cannot—by the nature of his research techniques—be considered the final word on the subject. However, they do correspond with certain traits of state politics, governments, and programs in a manner that lends weight to a cultural interpretation of state affairs. States that score high on Moralism and low on Traditionalism score high on voter activity and political competition and have a reformist record with respect to the character and procedures of their legislative and judicial branches. They have large numbers of state and local employees relative to population and high salaries and generous fringe benefits for government employees. These states also show an innovative record with respect to the introduction of new programs; they tend to have strong local governments; their tax payments are high relative to personal income; and they score high in their services for education, highways, and public welfare. Moreover, these findings are not simply the products of state economics. They appear no matter what the character of a state's economic indicators.[19]

Many features of state policy draw their impetus from peculiarities of state politics and traditions, without reference to economic traits or widespread cultural patterns. Oklahoma is a state with a traditional culture and a conservative reputation, but generous payments for public assistance. Oklahoma is not a rich state, so its welfare payments do not reflect abundant resources. Oklahoma's per capita expenditure for public welfare was $105.67 in 1974, while the national median was $84.43. In the neighboring—and wealthier—state of Texas, per capita spending was $67.43. What accounts for Oklahoma's peculiarity? The easiest explanation focuses on Oklahoma's sales tax. When the 2 percent levy was introduced in 1933, its proceeds were earmarked for the newly devised public welfare programs. As any reader of John Steinbeck's *Grapes of Wrath* recalls, Oklahoma suffered more than average during the Depression. One of its responses was to couple the new Federal welfare money with the income from its new sales tax. The result today is that Oklahoma's Welfare Department is guaranteed a lucrative annual revenue. Unlike its counterparts in most other states, it does not fight for its share of general tax funds during each budget session of the legislature. Quite the contrary, the department receives more revenue than is felt necessary for the public assistance programs alone. Rather than give up the earmarked tax (and risk skimpy budgets from a legislature that is no longer preoccupied with dust storms and hungry Okies), the Welfare Department has taken on functions that are assigned to other departments in most other states. The welfare budget in Oklahoma not only supports generous payments to the recipients of public assistance, but also pays for children's hospitals, prenatal care, and vocational rehabilitation.

Alabama is another low-income state that shows unusual support for some public assistance. Alabama does not provide the wholesale generosity of Oklahoma, but favors two of the assistance programs far more than others. Alabama scores where expected (well below the national averages) for most payments. The state's economy is poor, and its population takes a conservative view toward the support of people who do not provide for their own needs. These factors of sparse resources and low service motivations seem to account for the low level of benefit payments given to the permanently and totally disabled and, particularly, the families of dependent children. However, the blind and recipients of old age assistance do relatively well. The figures show that payments to the blind and to "pensioners"—as the old age recipients are labeled in Alabama—rank closest to the national average.[20]

Alabama Average Benefits, as Percentages
of National Averages, 1973–1974

OAP: 96%   AFDC: 44%   AB: 99%   APTD: 72%

There are other signs that Alabama treats its aged poor relatively well. The program's name—Old Age Pensions—is designed to remove some of the welfare onus from recipients. In order to provide financial security to the old age pensioners, the Alabama legislature has earmarked portions of six state taxes to the pension fund. The Old Age Pension program has received almost 80 percent of its total revenues from earmarked sources: liquor store profits and taxes on retail sales, whiskey, beer, cigarettes, and franchises. No other public assistance program in the state has received more than a pittance from earmarked sources. Alabama politicians respect the OAP program. Candidates for the governor's office generally advocate increases in benefits, and the eligibility requirements are liberal. Although a conservative governor (Persons) successfully sponsored a law in the early 1950s that required families of OAP recipients to be responsible for some of their support, Jim Folsom made this an issue in his next gubernatorial campaign and repealed the law during the 1955 session of the legislature. Alabama's interest in assistance for the aged is particularly noticeable when the OAP program is compared to the AFDC program. The figures above show that old age pensioners' benefits are more than twice as high (relative to national averages) as benefits for dependent children. Other data show the incidence of OAP recipients is almost three times higher than AFDC; this suggests that eligibility requirements are most liberal for OAP.[21]

Alabama Average Recipient Rates, as Percentages
of National Averages, 1973–1974

OAP: 233%   AFDC: 85%   AB: 167%   APTD: 100%

Alabama has also responded quickly to new Federal grants in behalf of the elderly. When several new features of Federally aided public assistance were enacted by Congress during the early 1960s, Alabama scooped up a program to pay for the nursing home care of its pensioners, but passed over an opportunity to aid the dependent children of unemployed parents.

Wisconsin merits recognition in any discussion of state programs. Its reputation dates from the progressive administrations of Governor Robert M. LaFollette: 1901-1906. Wisconsin was the first state with a modern personal income tax, in 1911; nine other states and the national government copied its tax procedures within a decade. Today Wisconsin ranks high in its reliance on income taxation and the continued willingness of its population to pay heavy taxes of several kinds. Per capita state and local tax revenue was eighth in the nation during 1973-1974, despite Wisconsin's below-average ranking in per capita personal income. A study of public opinion made by Louis Harris in 1958 found Wisconsin's residents better informed on public issues than those in other states and far more willing to support government programs with high taxes. Harris discovered that only 1 Wisconsin person in 10 felt that taxes were too high, and that only 1 in 20 wanted reductions in the Federal income tax. In contrast, over one-half of the people interviewed in Indiana and 40 percent of those in Ohio felt that taxes were too high.[22]

Wisconsin ranks higher than predicted on the basis of its economic resources in programs for education, welfare, highways, and natural resources.[23] The University of Wisconsin consistently ranks among the most prestigious in the country, and it attracts strong financial support from the Federal government and private citizens. The state provides leadership in such diverse fields as worker's compensation and corrections. Beginning in 1913 Wisconsin permitted certain prisoners to leave their institutions during the daytime hours for education or employment. Many states are still innocent of this reform in the 1970s, while elsewhere it is a recent innovation.

Louisiana also deserves attention for unusual policies. Not only does Louisiana pay much higher welfare benefits than are commensurate with its economic position, but makes its highest payments in the poorest counties. Louisiana's record in public welfare goes back to the administrations of the *second* Governor Long (Earl, who first served in 1939-1940). Earlier, Governor Huey Long set the state going in public services with huge investments in free school textbooks (for both parochial and public school children); in Louisiana State University (where the football team and band as well as academic departments and the personal funds of a corrupt president benefited from the largess); in public hospitals; and roads and bridges.[24] Public generosity in Louisiana is not explained solely on the basis of altruism. While the poor do benefit from government programs far more than in other Southern states, there are also some payoffs for the state's politicians. Huey Long's free spending helped other officials besides the LSU president. There is still a tendency for welfare recipients to balloon in number during the months before a state election.

Mississippi shows unusual resourcefulness in the design of its tax programs. It invented the modern retail sales tax in 1933 to reap sizable revenues despite the severe depression. The state sold mil tokens that merchants collected on even the smallest purchase. The tax did not win the applause of the nation's liberals who saw it as a regressive levy (i.e., because it takes a higher portion of low incomes than of middle and upper incomes). Yet it received widespread applause from other state governments. It was copied by 21 of them during the 1930s, and it is now used by 45 of the states. Mississippi's invention is the largest single source of revenue for state governments. In 1974 it accounted for $23 billion and about 30 percent of total state tax funds.

Mississippi's creativity in the field of taxation is evident in other programs besides the sales tax. For many years the state was dry of legal alcohol, but collected sizable funds on a bootleg liquor tax. This was paid by the liquor wholesalers of New Orleans and Memphis, who reported to Jackson on the alcohol they shipped into the state. With this device, Mississippi's politicians could maintain the prohibition that voters seemed to demand, yet profit from the inevitable consumption. Moonshine retained its privileged tax position, however, since the bootleg tax applied only to the "legal" alcohol ("red" lightning) coming illicitly from across the border.

Mississippi's version of the personal income tax demonstrates that a jurisdiction can bend a widely used device to suit its own policy preferences. In most states the personal income tax is progressive in taking a higher portion from the incomes of middle- and upper-level families than from the incomes of the poorest families. But this is not so in Mississippi. State officials look upon a progressive income tax as a deterrent to industrial development, and they have taken several steps to reduce the burden on high-income people. As of 1974 the tax included only two rates: 3 percent to $5,000 of taxable income and 4 percent above $5,000. Over $5,000 the tax rate does not increase and "progressivity" stops. Until recently, Mississippi allowed a personal deduction for a spouse, but none for children. This feature maximized the impact of the income tax on husbandless females having several children. A reader can judge if this tax reflected the merit of the Federal system or simply reflected the diversity of political mores that provides continuing support for the Federal system.

SOME NEED FOR FEDERAL COORDINATION

The Federal nature of American government permits state governments to act in their own citizens' interest. The benefit is apparent when states experiment in their programs and create more attractive efforts than expected from states of their type. One disadvantage comes when the self-interests of different states are competitive. Without a national government strong enough or wise enough to provide inducements or controls for common action, the neighboring states may get in each other's way.

Where different jurisdictions must agree on a program of pollution control, for example, upwind industrialists may use their state governments to protect them from downwind citizens. Why should New Jersey force its industries to increase expenditures for pollution-control devices in order to clean New York's air? Welfare checks are less generous in some states than elsewhere. Low-tax havens may appeal to some residents, but they are a burden to others who might otherwise receive better services. Even the simple matter of road and bridge construction may be delayed—or may falter altogether—because of the problems created by different state governments. Many of our largest cities sit astride state borders and create numerous problems of service coordination. New York, Philadelphia, Chicago, St. Louis, Memphis, Omaha, Kansas City, Cincinnati, and Louisville endure one Federal crisis after another in their pursuit of clear water, clean air, coordinated traffic control, and the multiple problems of citizens who live in one state but work in another: Where do they pay taxes? Where do the kids go to college and get the benefits of state residents' tuition? Where are they counted for purposes of allocating Federal aids?

One issue between Connecticut and Rhode Island illustrates some not-so-hidden problems when different state governments lend their weight to their residents' demands. The issue concerned the construction of an improved highway from New London, Connecticut to Providence, Rhode Island. Two routes presented themselves, as shown in Figure 2-2. The northern route appealed to Connecticut because it promised to bring new industries to the depressed towns in its northeast. The southern route appealed to Rhode Island because it would connect New York, Providence, and Boston with the tourist areas along Rhode Island's shore. The solution provided incomplete benefits to each state and wrought misery and danger to those who would traverse the entire route: Connecticut built its road along the northern route to the Rhode Island border, and Rhode Island built its highway along the southern route to the Connecticut border! Discontinuity prevailed for another half-dozen years until Connecticut built a connecting road between New London and southern Rhode Island. In the interim a motorist or trucker could select an interstate highway north from New London and then 30 miles of poorly maintained road until reaching Providence, or an interstate highway south from Providence and then 30 miles of two-lane road until reaching New London.

Federal efforts should smooth problems of coordination among state governments, but often produce further confusion. The regional offices of major Federal agencies illustrate the point. Ideally, they would help to coordinate efforts among neighboring states, at least in those programs that are aided by national funds. Yet the regional offices themselves are targets of competition among officials of state and local governments. For a city to capture one of these offices is something of an economic prize. Altogether, the field offices employ about 90 percent of the Federal civilian employees. They offer steady payrolls to the cities that serve as regional headquarters, plus a stream of visitors who patronize local hotels and restaurants. Congress and the Administration have spread these benefits to a large number of cities. Many agencies have had their major Southern office in Atlanta, while others have used Jacksonville, Charlotte, (N.C.), Charlottesville, (Va.), Knoxville, Richmond, or Birmingham. The Northeastern office of an agency may be in New York, Boston, or Philadelphia. Chicago, St. Louis, or Kansas City may house the Midwestern office, and Western offices may be anywhere between Dallas and Seattle. The problem comes when state or city officials must visit separate regional centers to negotiate a related set of projects that involve separate Federal agencies. The regional offices were conceived initially to save these officials a trip to Washington. Now, however, they may have to travel a circuit that is

Figure 2-2

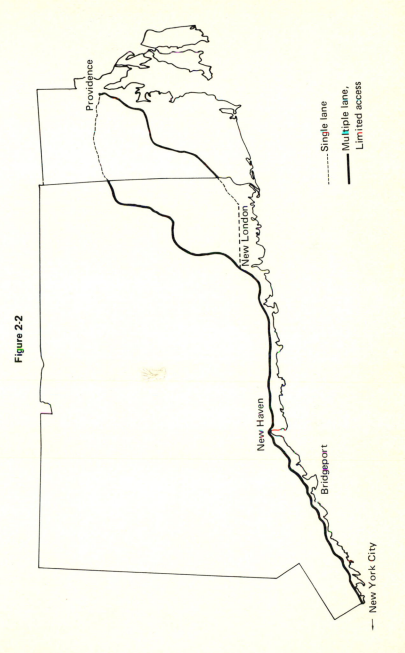

Providence

New London

New Haven

Bridgeport

New York City

------- Single lane

━━━ Multiple lane,
Limited access

47

three times as far and keeps the key Federal personnel far enough apart to complicate any effort to coordinate their programs.

The state of Kentucky and its subdivisions, for example, has been served by the regional offices of HUD in Atlanta, Georgia; HEW in Charlottesville, Virginia; the Bureau of Employment Security (Labor) in Cleveland, Ohio; the Bureau of Work Programs (Labor) and OEO in Washington, D.C.; EDA (Economic Development Administration) in Huntington, West Virginia; and state offices of Agriculture in Kentucky. A representative of the Executive Office of the President—or anybody else—could not call an interdepartmental regional meeting to consider a common approach to a problem or project in Kentucky without bringing people in from half a dozen localities—people who, when the meeting was over, would again scatter to cities spread across a third of the country.[25]

Only in 1969 did President Nixon face the problem of local competition for regional offices and formulate a common set of subcapitals for certain Federal units. Even then, however, there remained anomalies in the regional structure of the Federal government. Only five agencies (Labor, HEW, HUD, OEO, and the Small Business Administration) were affected by the President's order to relocate their ten regional offices into the same cities.

Finally, there are problems of public services that differ markedly from one state and region to another. The variation appears in virtually all programs. While some states offer mass higher education of a quality that rivals that of the prestigious private universities, others offer overcrowded facilities with thin academic programs. Welfare payments in the most generous of the wealthy states are far above those in the most conservative of the poor states. How much of this is the fault of the states themselves, and how much is it the responsibility of the national government? We return to this problem in Chapter 5. The differences among the states present both vexing problems and signs of hope. One's conclusions depend partly on political perspective and on the states that are under examination. For many of their failings, however, there are matching failings in the absence of Federal stimuli for better performance.

NOTES

1   See Reg Murphy, "The Maddox Administration Is Perhaps the Most Liberal in Georgia's History," *New York Times Magazine*, November 24, 1968, pp. 60 ff.

2   This section borrows heavily from my *Regionalism in American Politics* (Indianapolis: Bobbs-Merrill, 1970), pp. 168 ff.

3   See Robert Highsaw, "The Southern Governor: Challenge to the Strong Governor Theme," *Public Administration Review*, 19 (1959), pp. 7–11.

4   See also Frank Jonas, *Western Politics* (Salt Lake City: University of Utah Press, 1961), p. 4.

5   John Fenton, *Midwest Politics* (New York: Holt, 1966), p. 225.

6   See, for example, Douglas D. Rose, "National and Local Forces in State Politics," *American Political Science Review*, 67 (December 1973), pp. 1162–1173; the correspondence between Thomas R. Dye and Douglas D. Rose in the *American Political Science Review*, 68 (September 1974), pp. 1264–1265; and the correspondence involving William Lyons, David R. Morgan, John Wanat, Phillip W. Roeder, and Douglas D. Rose in the *American Political Science Review*, 70 (March 1976), pp. 159–174.

7   *Regionalism*, chap. 6.

8   *Regionalism*, pp. 92–97.

9   Norval D. Glenn and J. L. Simmons, "Are Regional Differences Diminishing?" *Public Opinion Quarterly*, 31 (Summer 1967), pp. 176–193.

10 *Regionalism*, pp. 81–92.

11 Daniel J. Elazar, *American Federalism: A View from the States* (New York: Thomas Y. Crowell, 1966), chap. 4.

12 Elazar, *American Federalism*, pp. 100–101.

13 See Harry M. Caudill, *Night Comes to the Cumberlands: A Biography of a Depressed Area* (Boston: Little, Brown, 1963).

14 This section relies on my *The Routines of Politics* (New York: Van Nostrand Reinhold, 1970), chap. 6.

15 Jack L. Walker, "The Diffusion of Innovations among the American States," *American Political Science Review*, 63 (September 1969), pp. 880–899.

16 Strictly speaking, it is inaccurate to say that current research measures the *influence* that certain elements exercise over policies. The closest we come to causation is the discovery of relationships that are consistent with causal patterns. If we hypothesize that

element *A* brings about policy *B*, we can infer support for that hypothesis if we find element *A* and policy *B* typically associated together in the same time and place. Of course, we must determine if the coexistence of *A* and *B* are due to some common trait *C* that might cause both *A* and *B* to occur together. There are techniques to "control" the primary relationships for underlying traits that might produce a correspondence between *A* and *B*. One hypothesis, for example, contends that high levels of political participation bring about generous levels of public service. If we find that states showing high citizen participation also show generous levels of public service, we have superficial support for the hypothesis. But we must check other explanations for the findings. It might be that the level of economic well-being influences both political participation and the generosity of public services. We know that people who are wealthy and well educated show more than the average amount of interest in politics, and we know that wealth has something to do with the resources needed to support public services. So the amount of economic wealth in a state may lead it to have high (or low) levels of political participation and corresponding levels of generosity in public services. See in particular, Thomas R. Dye, *Politics, Economics and the Public: Policy Outcomes in the American States* (Chicago: Rand McNally, 1966); and Herbert Jacob and Kenneth N. Vines, *Politics in the American States* (Boston: Little, Brown, 1971).

17 Sharkansky, *Regionalism*, Chapter 6.
18 Elazar, *American Federalism*.
19 See Ira Sharkansky, "The Utility of Elazar's Political Culture: A Research Note," *Polity*, 2 (September 1969), pp. 66–83; Edward J. Clynch, "A Critique of Ira Sharkansky's 'The Utility of Elazar's Political Culture,' " *Polity*, 52 (September 1972), pp. 139–141; Leonard G. Ritt, "Political Cultures and Political Reform: A Research Note," *Publius: The Journal of Federalism* (Winter 1974), pp. 127–133; and Charles J. Johnson, "Political Cultures in American States: Elazar's Formulation Examined," *American Journal of Political Science*, 20 (August 1976).
20 Ira Sharkansky, *Spending in the American States* (Chicago: Rand McNally, 1968), pp. 138–141.
21 The figures are recorded as OAP: number of recipients relative to the population over 65 years of age. For all other programs, the figures represent the number of recipients relative to the size of the total population. The source is *U.S. Statistical Abstract, 1975* (Washington: U.S. Government Printing Office, 1975).

22 Fenton, *Midwest Politics*, pp. 66–67.
23 Ira Sharkansky and Richard I. Hofferbert, "Dimensions of State Policy," in Jacob and Vines, *Politics in the American States*.
24 See T. Harry Williams, *Huey Long* (Boston: Little, Brown, 1970).
25 James L. Sundquist, *Making Federalism Work* (Washington: Brookings, 1969), p. 276.

Chapter 3

The Financial Muscle of State Governments

Mississippi, Louisiana, Kentucky, West Virginia, and Vermont usually appear on the bottom of state rankings. They are known for poverty, cultural backwardness, political leaders who are more quaint than tolerable, plus provincial—and worse—attitudes toward minority ethnic groups. For those who comment on race, Mississippi provides limitless examples of Americans' inhumanity to one another. West Virginia is the place where state officials aid the mineowners in their efforts to exploit the land and the people. Vermont is the land of stodgy Yankees, more cows than people, and diminishing population. Louisiana and Kentucky offer rustic, gallus-snapping politicians who preserve ancient customs by purchasing votes at the forks of the creeks and along the bayous.

It would be foolhardy for any advocate of the states to overlook these stereotypes. There is some truth in each one. But there are other sides to these states. They all try hard to support public services by taxing their citizens at rates substantially above the national averages. In a recent 1-year period when the Federal government's support for domestic activities wavered in the face of international commitments, Mississippi and Kentucky each increased their own tax collections by about 25 percent. It may be true that important actors in these states do not conform to certain standards of the twentieth century. Nonetheless, these states deserve recognition for some accomplishments. And theirs are the accomplishments of the poorest states! Many other state governments make commendable use of their more bountiful resources.

The central link in the argument that state governments deserve a better assessment is their record in providing financial support for public services. The states' financial muscle appears in their consistent and increasing portion of all governments' support of domestic programs. The states have remained strong when other governments weakened. The states held up their share during the Depression when some local authorities failed along with their real estate tax base. More recently the states have assumed an increasing portion of state-local responsibilities as the property tax again came under pressure. The states also took some responsibilities that had been the national government's as a larger portion of Washington's budget went to the Defense Department and our allies.

It is not just the well-heeled progressive states that assume more of all governments' financial burdens. Quite the contrast. Several states that are poor economically and suffer the most from liberal commentators have far larger budgets than expected on the basis of their resources. It is the Southern states and the poorer states elsewhere that carry a higher than average portion of the state-plus-local government budgets and tax above average percentages of their residents' personal income.

THE RECORD OF STATE FISCAL STRENGTH

This is not the easiest chapter for the general reader. It has more than its share of financial data and calculations. Any discussion of money is inherently quantitative, and a discussion of money is central to an understanding of which governments do what. In order to appraise the financial performance of state governments, we look at their record over the full range of the twentieth century. Before we begin, however, we must agree on some rules of measurement. *Inflation, increases in population,* and *increases in economic resources* all distort the meaning of government expenditures. If this chapter failed to take account of changes in population and the economy, it would overlook the obvious facts that state spending in raw dollars increases partly because a growing clientele demands more of the established services, partly because inflation diminishes the productivity of each dollar spent, and partly because a growing economy makes it possible to increase expenditures without increasing the government's demands on available resources.

By correcting expenditures for population increases and inflation, it is possible to avoid a gross exaggeration of increases in spending. Between 1932 and 1975, state expenditures in uncorrected dollars increased by 5,478 percent: from $2.8 billion to $156.2 billion. However, this appearance of increase changes substantially after correcting for population growth and inflation. Expenditures per capita in constant dollars (in 1958 dollars) increased by only 490 percent: from $67.52 to $398.43. By calculating state expenditures as a percentage of gross national product (GNP), it is possible to ascertain changes in the demands they make on available resources. In these terms, spending increased by only 116 percent: from 4.8 percent of GNP in 1932 to 10.4 percent of GNP in 1975.

We also want to calculate changes in the responsibilities of state governments—as compared with those of national and local governments. To do this, we must take account of changes in the responsibilities of the Federal government. Otherwise, we would inflate the image of Federal "encroachment" upon the activities of state and local governments. In order to make year-by-year comparisons of Federal, state, and local expenditures on a basis that permits the identification of changes in the expenditures of each level of government for comparable purposes, we examine expenditures made for the functions pursued in common by all governments. These figures *exclude* expenditures for the peculiarly Federal responsibilities of international affairs, defense, space exploration, the postal service, veterans' benefits, and interest on the national debt. Federal expenditures for these functions have increased from 39 percent of the Federal budget in 1940 to 57 percent in 1975.[1] Tables 3-1 and 3-2 provide the record of government spending for periods that include the Depression; wartime periods of 1940–1946, 1950–1954, and 1965–1969; and three

Table 3-1   State Government Expenditures, 1902–1975

	Total expenditures per capita, constant dollars	As percentage of GNP
1975	$398.43	10.4
1969	255.94	8.0
1965	197.02	6.7
1954	138.00	5.1
1950	139.11	5.3
1946	92.43	3.4
1940	102.50	5.2
1932	67.76	4.9
1927	–	2.2
1902	–	1.1

Source: *Facts and Figures in Government Finance, 1975* (New York: Tax Foundation, Inc., 1975); and U.S. Bureau of the Census, *State Government Finances in 1975* (Washington: GPO, 1976).

periods of postwar reconversion. With this information we can judge the responses of state, national, and local governments to each event.

The periods of greatest increase in state spending are the Depression, the period after World War II, and the recent period of Vietnam after 1965. The period after World War II saw fat years for all American governments. Federal taxes reached great heights during the war, and they still provided huge funds in the immediate postwar period. State and local governments accumulated financial reserves during the war. Due to the scarcity of manpower and materials, they could not spend all their income. State and local governments deferred construction and maintenance programs, then spent their reserves to catch up after the war. War-induced increases in population also had their first impact on demands for schools during the late 1940s. Both public demands and governmental responses were high from 1946 to 1950.

The periods of Depression and Vietnam provide the best test of the states' financial muscle. During the Depression the state and national governments carried the burden of public services, while some local

Table 3-2   All Governments' Common-function
Spending, by Percentage Spent* by Each Level
of Government, 1902–1975

	1975	1969	1965	1954	1950	1946
National	37.6	31.4	30.8	32.0	38.0	41.5
State	48.2	47.9	43.9	38.6	37.3	30.2
Local	50.3	52.1	60.3	58.3	44.9	52.4

	1940	1932	1922	1913	1902
National	41.8	13.6	15.2	10.9	9.9
State	30.6	31.7	22.3	16.9	16.7
Local	45.4	66.5	69.6	76.8	78.7

Sources: U.S. Bureau of the Census, *Historical Statistics on Governmental Finances and Employment,* U.S. Census of Governments, 1967, Volumes 4, 5, and 6, Number 5 (Washington: GPO, 1969); and U.S. Bureau of the Census, *Governmental Finances in 1968–1969, and 1974–1975* (Washington: GPO, 1970 and 1976).

*Percentages sum to more than 100 because intergovernmental expenditures are counted twice: once for the granting level and once for the level of final expenditures. Presumably, each level acquires some control over the final product of the spending and thus should be credited with some of its support. Our concern in this table is not so much the position of national, state and local governments in any one year, but their changes relative to one another from one year to another.

governments joint private enterprises in bankruptcy, and local governments generally reduced their share of all governments' financing from 67 to 45 percent of the total. During the recent Vietnam buildup the states had even more of the show to themselves. While the local governments' share of the total budget for domestic services shrunk from 60 to 52 percent and the national government's share stayed about the same, the state's share increased from 44 to 48 percent. The states have continued to increase their share of domestic spending with the decline of the country's commitments to Southeast Asia. Now as never before in the twentieth century, state governments have crucial roles in their support of public services.

What brought about the recent increase in the states' share of government budgets? Part of the explanation lies in a repeat of a Federal pattern observed during World War II and Korea: a withdrawal of Federal aids from certain programs under the exigencies of military and international activities. During some years of World War II there was an actual decline in Federal aids to state and local governments. This pattern did not repeat itself so severely in the late 1960s. The Johnson Administration tried to pursue a war against domestic poverty at the same time that it fought the Vietcong. The result was a development of some new Federal aid programs (e.g., Model Cities) at the same time that others were cut back.[2] What concerns us is the cutback. Washington trimmed funding estimates in highways, education, public health, and medical research. State or local governments had to pick up the slack to protect the Federally aided programs. In many cases the programs endured with lower budgets or were phased out. Where some effort was made to replace the Federal contribution, it was more often the work of the state than the local government.

Increasing citizen demands for public service also help to explain the increasing role of the states during 1965–1975. Many demands came in the traditional state sectors. Higher education, in particular, became a major item of government expenditure by 1969. It competed with highways as the major single item in the states' budgets, with each taking about one-quarter of the totals. While total state budgets were going up by 68 percent between 1965 and 1969, their budgets for higher education went up by 100 percent.

More recently the big increase in state expenditures came in the area of public welfare. This spending went up by 116 percent during 1969–1973, compared with 49 percent for other programs. In part this reflected a shift in program responsibilities from local to state governments, growing activities in medical payments for the poor, and new outreach programs designed to inform potential clients of their benefits. Welfare remains a fluid area. As we note in Chapter 5, events subsequent to 1973 are shifting some financing from state to national levels.

Another explanation of the rising state budgets is the increasing demands of local governments. The cry of "property tax relief" sounds frequently throughout the land and influences the decisions of state officials. The tax on real property—which is the mainstay of most local governments—comes in for more criticism than any other major source of local, state, or Federal revenue. Its opponents are not limited to property owners who pay the tax directly. Renters also pay the tax indirectly as part of their rent.   Labor unions and other spokespersons for low-income renters oppose the property tax because of its demonstrated effects on the poor. Studies by economists find the local property tax to be the *most regressive* of our major taxes. In 1965 it was found to take an average 6.9 percent of the income of families under $2,000 of annual income and only 2.4 percent of the income from families with more than $15,000 of annual income.[3]

The burdensome nature of local property taxes makes itself felt in state capitals. Funds from some recent increases in state income and sales taxes are committed to local governments. Optimists hope that state funds will permit some decrease in local property taxes. More realistically, the state funds will keep the local taxes from going as high as they might otherwise. Since the end of World War II, the states' portion of state and local tax receipts has increased from 47 to 58 percent.

Not all states have taken over a substantial portion of service activities within their borders. A ranking of states on the percentage of state-local budgets funded with state money shows a range from Delaware (79 percent) to New Jersey (41 percent). Two patterns are evident. The role of the state government is greatest among Southern states and among low-income states. For one of these findings there is a historic explanation and for the other an explanation in political economy. For low-income Southern states, of course, the two explanations dovetail.

The tendency for low-income states to rely heavily on state-collected revenues is evident in Louisiana, North Carolina, South Carolina, and Vermont. There are numerous local governments in these states (especially rural counties) that are hard-pressed to support even a minimum level of public services with the economic resources that lie within their jurisdictions. Perhaps because many local authorities in these states must rely upon state aid, all local governments in these states are inclined to view the state government as a prime source of funds. It is easier for the legislature to pass a state aid bill if there is something in it for the constituents of all legislators. On the other side of the income scale, *local governments* in the well-to-do states of New York, New Jersey, Massachusetts, and California carry a *larger than average* share of state and local financing. Seemingly out of step with the general pattern is Delaware. This state has one of the highest levels of personal income per capita in the nation, but is also the heaviest user of state government revenues. In this trait, Delaware reflects the pattern of its Southern neighbors. Southern states have been centralized historically, owing in part to a colonial experience of diffuse population and a plantation economy that did not nurture the development of strong, autonomous towns. Even in the wealthiest Southern states, the state provides a large share of the state and local revenues.

THE SPECIAL STRENGTH OF LOW-INCOME STATES

Conventional wisdom suggests that high-income states should spend the most. It is already apparent, however, that state authorities carry a heavier than average portion of the state-local burden under low-income conditions. It is consistent with this finding that total state expenditures per capita are frequently *high* in states that score *low* on the features of industrialization, urbanism, average level of adult education, population density, and per capita personal income.[4] In one group of low-income states (per capita income average of $4,520) the average per capita state spending was $604 during 1974.[5] In contrast, the per capita state spending was only $447 in a group of upper-income states (average income of $5,563).[6]

Why do measures of social and economic resources stand in *inverse* relationship to state spending? The best explanation points to a process of compensation with the state government making up for the inability of local authorities to pay for public services under low resource conditions. Economic measurements reflect needs as well as resources, and the *needs* of localities in states scoring low in population and industrialization explain why low incomes and high state spending go together.

Part of the problem for local governments is their enforced reliance on a tax base (real property) that is dependent upon the local economy. Compared with localities, state governments have legal access to greater economic resources within their larger jurisdiction; they benefit from a more generous selection of Federal aids; and they have a more productive tax system to extract revenue from available resources. The state levies on personal income and retail sales tap the economy of the whole state. They redistribute funds from "have" to "have not" areas, and they remain more productive in the face of depressed economic conditions than the local property tax. Also, state authorities seem to be less timid than local authorities about driving away industry with higher taxes. The tax explanation for industrial locations is often exaggerated. There are lots of reasons for an industrialist to choose—or leave—a plant site that have nothing to do with taxes. An adequate labor supply, access to markets and transportation, and attractive public services are often more important than taxes. However, the problem of tax-conscious industries is most pressing at the local level, where a business can move from one municipality to the next and still draw on the same work force, suppliers, and markets.

The compensating nature of state government spending appears most clearly in a ranking of states on the basis of expenditures per $1,000 of residents' personal income. This measures the financial effort of residents in supporting the activities of state governments and the political efforts of state governments in paying for public services. During 1974 the highest-ranking states were—in order—Vermont, New Mexico, Mississippi, Louisiana and West Virginia.[7] States scoring lowest were Indiana, Missouri, New Jersey, Kansas, and Texas. The local governments of Vermont et al. rank low in spending while those of Indiana et al. rank high. Where there is a lot of money in the private economy, it is the local governments that spend it. Under conditions of economic constraint, the state governments come to the fore.

The capacity of poor states to move against the economic tides looks even more impressive when the American record is compared with the history of governments' spending in other countries.[8] One theory about government spending grew out of the British experiences through World War II. It is the work of two economists, Alan T. Peacock and Jack Wiseman, and finds increasing *central* government spending under crisis conditions. Their study of public expenditures in the United Kingdom finds that spending levels (defined as percentages of national product) remain stable for long periods of time and spurt upward or fall behind only in response to severe national trauma.[9] For Britain, these traumas were the First and Second World Wars. Although it is expected that spending would increase to meet the demands of the war effort, the wars themselves were not the only stimuli at work. The

British public tolerated tax increases and other methods of raising revenues (e.g., service charges and government bonds) as war measures, but the measures brought in more revenue than was needed for the wars per se. The crises permitted revenue—and expenditure—levels to be *displaced* upward. And after the crises the return of revenue levels was not to their prewar status.

> Expenditures may fall when the disturbance is over, but they are less likely to return to the old level. The state may begin by doing some of the things it might formerly have wanted to, but for which it had hitherto felt politically unable to raise the necessary revenues. At the same time, social disturbances may themselves impose new and continuing obligations upon a government, as the aftermath of the disturbance (for example, the provision by a government of war pensions), as the result of the government being obliged by the disturbance to assume functions that it cannot easily return to others (for example, the wartime provision by government of services formerly financed by private charity), and as a consequence of changed ideas induced or encouraged by the disturbance itself.[10]

Peacock and Wiseman also see a *concentration* effect associated with the upward displacement of public expenditures. Concentration takes place as the *central government assumes an increasing proportion of public expenditures.* In part, concentration reflects the development of new revenue sources that are central government taxes. Primarily, they enable the central government to provide for the costs of the war; and secondarily they provide the basis for expanded domestic services. Improvements in communication, transportation, and individual mobility that accompany wars may provide the incentive for making social services more uniform in their quality throughout the nation. The same improvements in communication and transportation make a central administration of public services more feasible. As war needs and the national emergency become prominent, local governments are more inclined to accept the growth of national institutions. Insofar as the war-induced domestic expenditures provide for services that government agencies had not provided before, the concentration at the center may proceed without threatening to remove established programs from the control of local authorities.

The Peacock-Wiseman theory of displacement and concentration does not fit the American experience of the twentieth century. It is possible to discern an upward displacement of all governments' spending during the First and Second World Wars, Korea, and Vietnam. But there is not prominent concentration of domestic expenditures at the Federal level. Perhaps the strong constitutional and political supports for state and local autonomy mitigate whatever temptations toward concentration lie within the crisis situation. The relative financial position of local governments in the United States enjoyed a resurgence after World War II. Localities improved their position from 33 percent of all governments' spending for domestic programs in 1944 to 60 percent in 1965. More recently, however, the localities' share has declined again. But now it is the state governments more than Washington that are showing increased responsibility for domestic budgets.

A reader might ask "Why should the poor states have to impose heavier than average tax burdens on their residents?" Would not a more rational Federal system transfer resources from wealthy to poor jurisdictions so that citizens across the country would receive tax bills and service outputs of roughly equal magnitudes? That would be nice, but it does not work that way. Many of the Federal grants-in-aid are designed to transfer resources from "have" to "have not" states, but they fall short of producing equality in either state tax burdens or state services. That they do not equalize conditions among the states is the result of decisions made by the Federal Administration and Congress. In the absence of any greater assistance from the Federal government, the poor states must continue taxing themselves severely.

WHERE DOES IT COME FROM? STATE RESPONSES
TO REVENUE DEMANDS

The ultimate source of the states' financial muscle is the pocketbooks of their citizens and the balance sheets of their corporations. The more direct sources—and those which shed light on the strength of state *governments*—are the revenue decisions made by state officials. In recent years, the state revenue story is one of persistent growth in kinds of revenues and in the amounts collected. Twelve states reinstituted state lotteries (a popular source of government revenue during colonial days), state parks that had been free began to charge admission fees, universities that had charged only modest student fees demanded sizable tuition, and more states borrowed heavily. By far the most prevalent revenue actions are those which create new taxes, expand the coverage of existing taxes, or increase the rates of the existing taxes. These require the most difficult political decisions. No politicians who are concerned about their future careers enjoy an upward change in tax policy, no matter how much they enjoy the opportunity to advertise improvements in public service that come along with their administration.

The recent history of Federal taxation sets the stage for a discussion of state tax policy. The Federal picture is one of stability or decline in the rates of most taxes. By 1944 Federal taxes were approximately in the form that still exists. A progessive tax on individual incomes was the single greatest source of revenue with lesser revenues produced by a corporate income tax. Far behind were levies for social security and excise taxes on gasoline, alcohol, and tobacco. The individual income tax remains dominant (49 percent of all Federal tax revenues during 1975), and it displays most clearly the decline in Federal tax rates that has occurred along with persistent growth in state taxation. After rate increases (and reductions in personal exemptions) that came as war measures during 1940–1947, the trend has been toward lower rates and larger personal exemptions. The only exceptions occurred during the Korean and Vietnam wars. Each of the wartime tax increases (and particularly the most recent) served not only to raise revenues but also to withdraw private purchasing power and put a brake on inflation.

The explanation of decline in the major Federal tax rates looks to the productivity of the income taxes. It is not so much a case of the national government shirking its revenue obligations, as the existing devices being able to produce large increments of funds that serve the needs of Congress and the Administration. The progressive rates of the Federal income taxes move people and firms to higher brackets during periods of economic prosperity and inflation. As anyone can discover by working through the International Revenue Service Form 1040, there are numerous steps in tax rates from the $500 to $100,000 income categories. Federal tax laws can stay the same yet produce considerable increases in revenue. Because of the progressive rate feature, the tax revenues increase faster than economic growth. Economists speak in shorthand and say that the *elasticity* of the Federal income tax is greater than 1.0. One of the great tax events of the 1960s was the demonstration that—under favorable economic conditions—a *reduction* in Federal tax rates could stimulate sufficient growth in private economic activity to produce an *increase* in public revenues.

An important contrast to this pattern of stable or reduced rates in the Federal income tax has occurred in the payroll tax that supports old age, survivors, disability, and hospital insurance. This tax has increased its rates from 1.5 percent of an employee's first $3,000 of income in 1950 to 5.85 percent of the first $13,200 in 1975. In the same period, the tax has increased its contributions to all Federal taxes from 6 to 24 percent. An effect of this change has been to make the entire Federal tax system less progressive, as individual and corporate income levies have declined from 72 to 66 percent of total Federal taxes.

Still members of Congress and administrators wax in relative fat and get into arguments over how to spend their resources. It is the plight of state politicians to scrounge for more funds. State taxes lack the elasticity of the Federal income taxes. In order to meet the demands for expenditures that are described earlier, the state governments must develop new taxes, expand existing ones, or increase existing tax rates. Over the past decade there has been a continuous record of new and enlarged state taxes. Between 1959 and 1970, there were 410 instances of new taxes or increased rates for the major state taxes on income, sales, and excises. During that period only three states escaped upward changes in the major taxes on incomes and retail sales, and only Louisiana (already a high-tax state) went through the period without an upward change in these or the excise taxes.

The revenue pinch was tight enough for several states to abandon long-held traditions against the enactment of certain taxes. The tobacco states of North Carolina and Virginia now tax cigarettes. Four states with a progressive bent in their politics (Massachusetts, Minnesota, New York, and Wisconsin) enacted sales taxes despite acrimonious debates in the press and the legislature. Nebraska and New Jersey entered the decade with *neither* an income nor a sale tax, but emerged with *both*.

Excise taxes on cigarettes and alcohol received the most attention from state legislatures. Tobacco and alcohol are vulnerable to taxation partly because they are "not good for us." Hopefully—according to one argument—a high tax provides an economic incentive for citizens to avoid injurious habits. Yet the taxes do not appear to dissuade consumers as much as they provide a lucrative flow of funds. During the 1959–1970 period 10 states enacted four separate increases in cigarette taxes, and Maine increased its tax five times! Four states made three separate rate increases in their taxes on alcohol and twenty states made two increases.

Not all states follow the same route of taxation. Although the recent period is marked by an eclectic pursuit of revenues wherever they seem available, there remain distinct traditions in the taxes that states prefer. An analysis of state tax policies in 1974 showed differences between one group of states that prefers income taxes and another group that prefers sales taxes. Yet another group of states (from among those favored by huge deposits of natural resources) collect large sums in severance taxes. Table 3-3 ranks the states that dominated in each category of tax emphasis.

In the 10 years since 1964, the states have sought to obtain more of the revenue benefits of progressive income taxes. Personal income levies went from 14 to 23 percent of state taxes, thus challenging the myth that the national government preempted this revenue source in the 1930s and 1940s.

The advantages touted by supporters of the personal income tax are its progressivity and elasticity. Of all the major taxes collected by state (and local) governments only the income tax (in most states)

Table 3-3 States Making Heavy Use of Specified Taxes, 1974

General sales	Income	Severance
Washington	Oregon	Louisiana
Indiana	New York	Texas
Hawaii	Minnesota	Oklahoma
Mississippi	Wisconsin	Alaska
South Carolina	Alaska	New Mexico

Source: Facts and Figures in Government Finance, 1975 (New York: The Tap Foundation, Inc. 1975).

avoids the onus of taking a bigger percentage bite from the incomes of poorer families than wealthier families. Partly because of this, it is the "income tax" states that show a tax elasticity greater than 1.0 (i.e., whose tax revenues automatically increase more than personal incomes during periods of prosperity).[11]

The sales tax remains the largest single source of state revenues, accounting for 30 percent of tax proceeds. Supporters of the sales tax claim it imposes fair charges on income groups that make the greatest use of public services, and that it does not take inordinate funds from the income classes who will benefit the economy by their investments. The state income tax takes an increasing portion of middle and upper incomes. Services, in contrast, tend to benefit lower-income families more than middle-and upper-income families.[12]

Such calculations pertain to all states' taxes and services taken together. They do not show the significant variations in tax or service policies from one state to another. It would be a mistake to assume that states choose either an income or sales tax and thereby proceed to common choices of its coverage, rates, and exemptions. There is much creativity in the field of tax policy. Thirty state governments make an effort to reduce the burden of their sales taxes on low-income families by exempting food and/or medicine from the levy. There is infinite variety in the coverage, rates, and exemptions used by the states having personal income taxes. Several states have some negative rates. These negative income taxes are meant to reimburse the poor for state or local sales or property taxes that are especially burdensome. Wisconsin's program for property tax relief provides the greatest relief to persons with the lowest income and phases out gradually for people with higher incomes. It aids those poor citizens who pay rent for homes or apartments by assuming that a certain portion of the rent is actually a contribution to the landlord's property tax. The program operates through the state income tax; the low-income citizens claim a property tax subsidy as a credit against their income tax. If their income tax is too low to be reduced by the total amount of their property tax relief, they get the remainder as a refund check from the State Department of Taxation.

Any discussion of creativity in tax policy must credit state governments for some of the most widely adopted inventions in the field. The modern era of income tax administration began in Wisconsin and Mississippi during 1911–1912 before the Federal government began its program in 1913. Wisconsin personnel moved to Washington and used their state-derived expertise to set up the Federal tax. During the next decade fifteen more states began individual or corporate income taxes—largely on the Wisconsin model. Mississippi invented the modern retail sales tax in 1932 to produce revenues during a period of economic depression that had crippled state and local property taxes and weakened the state income tax. Within a period of 6 years, 23 more states followed Mississippi's lead.

All states use their taxing authority to aid local governments. There are shared taxes and other forms of state financial aid. An increasing number of states permit local governments to tax retail sales and personal income (i.e., beyond the traditional bounds of the local property tax), with state revenue departments providing the administrative services of collection and audit for the local governments. States also monitor the property taxes of local authorities and take steps to keep property assessments reasonably equal from one community to another for properties of similar value. These topics deserve attention in a discussion of state efforts in the field of taxation. In this book, however, they belong in Chapter 6 along with other state efforts in behalf of local governments.

THE FINANCIAL MUSCLE OF STATE GOVERNMENTS: WHAT MOUNTAINS CAN IT MOVE?

This chapter assumes that high levels of government spending are a strength of state governments. The dollars provided in state budgets should affect the nature of public services. At the least, however, this assumption suffers from important limitations. No matter how much expenditures are welcomed by program advocates, they cannot determine by themselves the nature of public services.

To understand this point, it is helpful to think in terms of *policy delivery systems.* The end products of these systems are the programs of government, and—ultimately—their impacts on citizens' lives. State spending is one factor that goes into the policy delivery system to shape its products. However, state spending is only one of the inputs. In order to judge the influence of spending on public services, it is necessary to take account of some other components of the policy system.

Besides spending, the factors that influence public services are the nature of an agency's staff and its leadership, physical facilities, the clientele who are to be served, the organizational structure of the service agencies, and the political and economic environments that surround policy decisions.

The influence of government spending on public services is more often assumed than demonstrated. The belief is widespread that expenditures are the primary determinants of public services, but the hard evidence is scarce. Most writers who assume the spending-service correspondence fail to test their belief.[13] A highly regarded study of education finds that school spending bears little relationship to the learning that goes on in the school. More important are traits of the pupil's family and friends. If the pupil comes from a well-educated family and associates with chums who are academically motivated, then more success in school is likely than if the situations of family and friends are not supportive.[14] Other research finds that states spending a lot of money for highways, welfare, health, and public safety do not always have the most admired services in these fields.[15] The cliché that *spending produces services* seems less accurate than its counter cliché that *spending is not everything*.

Because the production of public services is a complex phenomenon that involves the interaction of many factors, it is difficult to see how the current level of public expenditure, by itself, will have overriding importance. Depending on the distribution of expenditures among the various claims within any service agency, a total budget may be used for any of numerous individual emphases: the salaries of newcomers or old-timers; new facilities; land acquisition; the repair and maintenance of equipment; auxiliary services; or any one of num erous program emphases. In the welfare field, a preoccupation with programs for the aged, blind, and disabled may consume a large budget at the expense of unwed mothers and their dependent children. In public education, an emphasis on academic instruction may get in the way of vocational education in ghetto neighborhoods.

We cannot say that the states' financial strength guarantees program success. First, money alone does not make public services. Secondly, some states are very poor. Even though Mississippi, Louisiana, North Dakota, and other low-income states tax their residents heavily in order to support state programs, there are severe limits to the available funds. In each of these states the state government itself carries almost all of the burden. Local governments are weak and do not produce the funds that they do in other states. Even where there are abundant resources, officials' ignorance about the true nature of service-determinants remains to hinder the policy delivery systems in the states. If financial resources represent some real *accomplishments* and *opportunities* of the states, some of their decision-making procedures remain as *problems*.[16] These problems are not only apparent in the states but appear in national and local governments as well.

Despite these problems, the financial efforts of state governments deserve praise for themselves. They attest to the creativity and the political courage of countless politicians. In numerous fields, moreover, the evidence is clear that state funds help to produce creditable programs. Perhaps the best record of the states is in the field of higher education. Other accomplishments appear in programs that are aided by the Federal government—in some cases *despite* frustrating and arbitrary regulations that come along with the Federal money. Still other accomplishments appear in recent state efforts in behalf of urban problems. More about all these programs in Chapters 4 to 6.

NOTES

1 See the discussion in my *The Politics of Taxing and Spending* Indianapolis: Bobbs-Merrill, 1969), pp. 29 ff.

2 An interesting anomaly appears in the comparison of Table 3-2 with Table 5-1 in Chapter Five. Table 3-2 shows state governments increasing their portion of all governments' support for domestic services, while the support of the Federal government for these services remained relatively constant up to 1969. Yet Table 5-1 shows an increasing portion of state funds coming from the Federal government. How could the Federal government become more dominant in state finances but not in the overall provision of domestic services? Increases in the Federal support for domestic services appeared to be concentrated in grants-in-aid to the states. Federal support of its own directly administered services (e.g., medical and other scientific research, agricultural supports and other natural resource activities) seemed to be declining relative to state programs.

3 "Allocating Tax Burdens and Government Benefits by Income Class" (New York: The Tax Foundation, Inc., 1967).

4 Ira Sharkansky, *Spending in the American States* (Chicago: Rand McNally, 1968), chap. 4.

5 This group includes Kentucky, Louisiana, Mississippi, Montana, New Mexico, North Dakota, Oklahoma, and Vermont.

6 This group includes Illinois, Indiana, Ohio, Missouri, New Jersey, and Texas.

7 This ranking omits Alaska and Hawaii due to the extreme pressures of inflation on incomes, taxes, and government expenditures in those states.

8 This discussion relies on *Taxing and Spending,* pp. 146 ff.

9 Alan T. Peacock and Jack Wiseman, *The Growth of Public Expenditure in the United Kingdom* (Princeton, N.J.: Princeton University Press, 1961).

10 Peacock and Wiseman, p. 27.

11 Advisory Commission on Intergovernmental Relations, *State and Local Finances: Significant Features 1967 to 1970* (Washington: GPO, 1969), p. 67.

12 "Allocating Tax Burdens and Government Benefits by Income Class" (New York: Tax Foundation, Inc., 1967).

13 This section relies on *Taxing and Spending*, chap. 6.

14 James S. Coleman, *Equality of Educational Opportunity* (Washington: GPO, 1966).

15 *Taxing and Spending,* chap. 6.

16 See my *The Routines of Politics* (New York: Van Nostrand Reinhold, 1970).

Chapter 4

Higher Education: Now the State Owns the Schoolhouse

Harvard, Yale, and Princeton are the bastions of age, social status, and academic prestige. For over 300 years their graduates have taken the top places in commerce, banking, law, medicine, government, religion, and literature. Their admissions officers turn away more high-ranking candidates than most other colleges can attract. The prospect of an acceptance or rejection quickens the pulse of mothers, sons, and now daughters in upper-middle-class suburbs all over the United States. During 4 years at one of these campuses a student is expected to associate with someone from a prominent family or with someone who will become prominent. Even if a graduate does not become great, he or she will at least know someone who does.

The Big Three and other institutions of the educational establishment no longer dominate the scene. For one thing, they are too small. Their graduates cannot possibly meet the needs for highly trained manpower in a dynamic economy. Second, they face increasing competition from institutions that were not open when Eastern colleges were 100 years old. Beyond the Appalachians the state universities draw on the taxing power of their legislatures to pay for high-priced faculty talent, equipment, and physical facilities across a range of academic programs whose breadth would break even the enviable endowments of the Ivy League. Schools like the University of California at Berkeley, Michigan, and Wisconsin provide leadership in the humanities and the physical, biological, and social sciences, and now can match or surpass the programs offered by the Big Three of the East.

From a social perspective, the greatest failing of the prestigious private institutions is their inability to accommodate vast increases in demand for higher education. To be sure, they have all increased their enrollments, and they have special programs for blacks and other students from culturally deprived backgrounds. Yet these efforts are pitifully small in size. If blacks, Latin Americans, American Indians, and poor white are to get a fair chance at higher education, it will come through the mass institutions created and financed by state governments. The new frontier of American education is not on the Charles or at Old Eli, but is at places like Los Angeles State College, Southern Illinois University, and Miami-Dade Junior College.

Of all the services that are supported by state funds, the state governments have most clearly taken command of higher education. Since World War II they have invested huge resources to meet the expanding demands in this field. In the 1930s, the bulk of higher education was provided by private colleges or universities. Now the greatest portion comes from public institutions.

This chapter is part of the argument that state governments play an increasing role in providing important public services. By itself the chapter cannot prove the point about the states. Higher education is only one of the states' services. Yet higher education is different from other services in that it promises vast future payoffs for individuals and communities. By assuming the responsibility for higher education, the states are doing more than just training students.

Here we examine the states at their best. They responded to increasing demands with expenditures that multiplied themselves one year after the next. Moreover, expanding support by the states came during years in the late 1960s that were made difficult by the economic pinch of rising taxes and reduced Federal support and by the political pinch of widespread student unrest.

There are six related and commendable developments in state-supported higher education. Each of them dates approximately from the end of World War II.

1 Development of new institutions
2 Increasing enrollments
3 Increasing variety in the programs offered
4 Improvements in the laboratories, libraries, and other facilities of higher education
5 Increases in faculty salaries
6 Improvements in the preentry training of faculty members and in their opportunities for continuing professional self-improvement

Each of these dimensions translates into greater opportunities for state residents and enhanced opportunities for basic changes in the American economy and culture. On each of these dimensions, moreover, state institutions have outstripped those in the private sector.

Changes in higher education have not come without difficulties. There has been turmoil as well as progress in higher education in recent years. The signs of friction are student riots, claims that too many faculty members concentrate on their own professional opportunities at the expense of their students, and now a glutted market for academic personnel. As in many kinds of diagnosis, however, it is difficult to tell the problems from the symptoms. If many faculty members are preoccupied with their own professional advancement, we may applaud the opportunities for research that are now available in magnitudes that were hardly perceived in the days before World War II. Not only physical scientists and specialists in agriculture and medicine, but faculty in the social sciences and humanities can now sharpen their own skills (and presumably improve their teaching) at the same time that they offer something of value to the culture at large. True, there is much dross in research. Too many books provide only ill-deserved promotion for their authors. Yet the creative process is mysterious and expensive. Important scientific and artistic efforts do not attract wide public attention. Works have been unrecognized for years before earning intellectual or economic success. The nagging criticisms of excessive faculty research and consulting are not without some merits. To evaluate these charges, however, we must also take account of the intellectual opportunities that are made available for students and society because of faculty research.

The glut in the academic market is another symptom that may have positive as well as negative meaning. Those who would criticize universities for producing too many Ph.D.s must also concede that they met the demands for more faculty members that dominated educational circles in the mid-1960s. It is also to the credit of the educational process that lots of bright young people finish their undergraduate careers with the desire to train for an academic profession. Certainly the salaries do not provide all the incentives that lure students into an academic life.

The academic glut could be temporary. Colleges can make good use of additional faculty despite a leveling off of the student population. A lower student-faculty ratio is helpful in several aspects of the educational process. Many legitimate student complaints about inattention from their instructors would be met by hiring more teachers for a fixed number of pupils. The increasingly specialized nature of the academic disciplines (which can be viewed positively as a sign of increasing knowledge about our world) can absorb more talent to provide instruction and carry on research in each of the specialties. The end of the Vietnam war, increased Federal moneys for domestic programs, and the freeing of state money could have provided the smaller classes that have always been the educator's preference. By and large, great additional resources have not come to higher education in the most recent years. Neither public nor private institutions have exploited the glut of academic personnel in this fashion. Yet many institutions have acted responsibly by shifting resources from the training of Ph.D.s to undergraduate instruction.

As in other fields of public service, there are considerable variations from state to state in the programs of higher education. State universities in California, Wisconsin, and Michigan have long been ranked with the most prestigious of the private universities, and they now provide models for other states to follow. California's model, in particular, is pursued by numerous states. It has three components:

1   At least one major institution in the state that provides a wide range of graduate instruction, subsidizes faculty research, and admits the best of the high school graduates

2   Several 4-year institutions to concentrate on baccalaureate level education and limited masters' programs in education and business

3   Many 2-year institutions within commuting distance of virtually every resident of the state to provide programs in vocational training and the equivalent of freshman and sophomore liberal arts programs.

Several public universities in the South reflect the expansions that are evident in other fields of public service throughout that region. Public universities in the Northeast, in contrast, remain mostly in the shadow of well-established private institutions. Despite vast increases in their own programs, New Jersey, Connecticut, New York, and Pennsylvania still ranked 45th, 47th, 48th and 50th in per capita state spending for higher education during 1974.[1]

THE CHANGING NATURE OF HIGHER EDUCATION

The most prominent changes in higher education are great increases in magnitude and the states' takeover of a service that was provided earlier by the private sector.

First, some information about the growth in higher education, including both public and private sectors. There are more students, more institutions, and more diverse opportunities for students in an expanding number of specialties. Between 1939 and 1973 enrollments in American institutions of higher education increased by more than seven times: from 1.3 million to 9.6 million. The increase in enrollment far outstrips the increase in population during the same period. Since the mid-1950s, higher education enrollment has climbed from 28 percent of the 18–21 year age group to 60 percent of this age group. It is not just that there are more clients for higher education. The clients come from different backgrounds and assert different demands than in the past. Many students in higher education come from ethnic and class origins that virtually would have disqualified them for advanced education a few years ago. Others pursue careers that were not served earlier by higher education. To accommodate these students, higher education has changed at the same time that it has grown. The greatest changes appear in those sectors that produce professional and technical personnel: graduate schools and junior colleges. Their enrollment increases were more than two and four times those of 4-year institutions over the 1940-1973 period. Since 1968, most of the growth has occurred in 2-year institutions. Their enrollment grew by 66 percent during 1968–1973, while that of graduate institutions grew by 25 percent and 4-year institutions by 22 percent. Institutions have also increased in number, but not as rapidly as enrollment. There were about 33 percent more institutions in 1974 than in 1960. Most of the new schools have been junior colleges.

Growths in enrollments and institutions tell us several things about higher education. There are more people being served today; there are more institutions; and the average institution is serving more students. These changes suggest problems in the governance of higher education. The educational process has, presumably, become less personal. There are lots of new faculty as well as new students. With expansion in the number of institutions, there are lots of new deans, presidents, and trustees. Students, faculty, administrators, and trustees have expressed discontent about one another's behavior. At least some of this discontent may reflect problems of internal control that are endemic in new or expanding operations.

More serious problems appeared on the campuses from the context of the larger society. The late 1960s and early 1970s saw a heady increase in political activism and no little violence. Most prominent were protests against the war in Southeast Asia. Lyndon Johnson's withdrawal from the 1968 campaign was attributable at least partly to campus-centered challenges to his policies. Campus rage reached even greater heights 2 years later with the invasion of Cambodia, suggesting some limits to the effective power of the protesters over substantive policy. Other protests focused on campus issues derived from larger domestic struggles: the greater recruitment of ethnic minorities and women to student bodies and faculties, and the development of academic programs focused on blacks, Hispanic-Americans, native Americans, other ethnic groups, and women.[2]

Improvements in faculty preparation and faculty salaries should produce better education. An instructor with an advanced degree is, presumably, better prepared and thus a better teacher than a colleague without an advanced degree. Higher salaries should attract into the academic professions a higher proportion of those bright and skillful people who are motivated at least partly by economic considerations. Looking just at universities offering advanced graduate degrees, there was an increase of 37 to 54 in the percentage of their faculties having doctorate degrees over the 1950–1966 period. There were comparable increases for the faculty of 4-year colleges, although at a lower range: from 27 to 38 percent with doctorates. There was also good news about faculty salaries from 1960 to 1968, but some disappointments thereafter. In the earlier period, salaries increased some 35 percent more than the cost of living. From 1968 to 1974, however, the cost of living increased 2 percent more than salaries.

Higher education deserves some credit for expanding its output of professional skills. There were about 46,000 masters' and doctors' degrees awarded in 1947–1948 and 285,000 in 1974. Moreover, graduate students were taking a bigger slice of resources in higher education. The advanced degrees increased from 14.4 percent of the total degrees awarded in 1947–1948 to 23.4 percent of the total awarded in 1974. If there is a spillover from graduate to undergraduate education, our colleges should be more sophisticated in the whole range of their offerings.

THE GROWING STATE ROLE IN HIGHER EDUCATION

What have the states done for higher education? The state governments are responsible for most of its growth. The private institutions held 51 percent of total enrollment in the early postwar year of 1947, but public institutions had 76 percent by 1973. State expenditures in their own institutions of higher education went from 42 percent of all higher education spending in 1950 to 45 percent in 1972. The increase would be even larger if it included state support for private institutions or state loans and scholarships given directly to the students of public and private institutions.

The public sector's role in higher education appears strongest if we take account of increasing subsidies given to private institutions by state governments. A summary measure of state involvement in higher education is the total spent by all state governments for that service; this includes direct appropriations for state institutions, state aids to locally supported institutions, subsidies to private schools, and scholarships, loans, and other direct aids to students at both public and private colleges. For 1973–1974 the sum for all 50 states was $15.4 billion. This compares with about $3.5 billion spent for higher education by local governments and about $5.9 billion by the Federal government.

State governments aid private institutions in several ways. Formerly private Temple University and the University of Pittsburgh are now defined as state-related, and received an annual state appropriation for operating expenses of about $80 million in 1969–1970. Elsewhere in Pennsylvania a total of 14 schools labeled "private: state aided" received $22.4 million in 1969–1970. These range from the Ivy League University of Pennsylvania ($12 million) to the Pennsylvania College of Optometry ($84,000). In Milwaukee, Marquette University divested itself of a medical college so that the state could pay without violating a constitutional prohibition against the support of church-related institutions. In New York, the state took over the University of Buffalo lock, stock, and tenured faculty. It now is the State University of New York at Buffalo and is prominent among the S.U.N.Y. campuses that support research and advanced graduate training.[3]

The Federal government's contribution to higher education comes principally from the Department of Health, Education, and Welfare but also from the Defense Department, the Department of Housing and Urban Development, the National Science Foundation, the Veterans Administration, and a scattering of other donors. In recent years the Federal government has shifted its priorities from graduate and professional education to 2-year colleges. Between 1973 and 1977, 2-year colleges increased their take from 22 to 34 percent of Federal contributions. Receipts of graduate and professional institutions declined in the same period from 22 to 16 percent of Federal aids.

There are still sizable national funds going to elite institutions. In 1972, $2.7 billion went to 100 institutions. Massachusetts Institute of Technology (a private institution) retains its number 1 ranking. State institutions are prominent in the top 10: the Universities of Washington (2), Michigan (3), Minnesota (5), California at Los Angeles (6),

Wisconsin-Madison (7), and California at San Diego (10). The remaining private schools in this group are Harvard (4), Stanford (8), and Columbia (9).

Just as there is public money going to private institutions, so there is private money going to public institutions. It is to the credit of several state universities that they attract contributions from their alumni, business firms, and private foundations over and above their considerable receipts in state taxes. In 1971-1972, the Universities of California and Texas ranked in fourth and fifth places among institutions with large private support. They received $36 million and $33 million, respectively. In states like Michigan, California, Texas, and Wisconsin the public universities have the attractions of prestige and excellence in their states that has been acquired nationwide by Harvard, Yale, and Princeton. Likewise, these state institutions share with the elite private schools the burdens of prominence. Just as conservative parents in Massachusetts steer their children away from allegedly red classrooms in Cambridge, so conservative parents in other parts of the country steer their children away from Ann Arbor, Madison, Austin, and Berkeley.

Increased opportunities for higher education are measured not only in state-supported institutions, enrollments, faculty, and expenditures, but also in the relatively low fees charged to students. It is no surprise that costs are rising at both public and private institutions: tuition and room and board estimates more than doubled during the 1965-1975 period. Also, it is well known that charges at the public schools are lower than at the private schools. The differences are sharpest for tuition but also appear for room and board. What is surprising is the more rapid increase in costs at private than public institutions. During 1957 estimated costs for tuition and room and board at public schools were 55 percent of those at private schools; in 1975 the costs at public schools were only 46 percent of those at private schools. This difference may reflect the greater economies of scale at the larger public schools. In any case, financial inducements are leading potential students increasingly in the direction of public institutions. Growth in the numbers of institutions, enrollments, and faculty complement the picture. Public higher education is growing in magnitude and quality, but it is costing less in relation to the private alternative.

QUALITY IN STATE HIGHER EDUCATION

What about the product that students get for their money? Comparisons between the quality of public and private institutions are more controversial than comparisons between size, numbers of institutions, numbers of faculty, and state expenditures. Faculty salaries and the incidence of faculty members with advanced degrees provide some clue to improvements in the quality of state institutions. On both items, public institutions have shown more improvement than private institutions in recent years. A study made in 1954 found 37 percent of the faculty in private institutions with doctorates but only 36 percent of the faculty in public institutions. By 1966 the proportions of doctorates among the faculties in both kinds of institutions had increased, but the ratio now slightly favored public institutions: 48 percent to 46 percent. In the numerical increase of faculty with doctorates, the public institutions greatly outgrew the private institutions: an increase of 47,400 doctorates over the 12-year period for public schools as opposed to an increase of 19,000 for private schools. The information for faculty salaries varies with academic rank and the kind of institution. Just looking at salaries in public and private universities over the 1961-1962 to 1968-1969 period, the following differences in percentage increases for the major ranks appear.

	Public, %	Private, %
Professor	+51.7	+48.0
Associate Professor	+50.5	+46.0
Assistant Professor	+49.7	+42.6

In each of these classifications, the growth in salary has been greater in the public than in the private sector.

The measurement of quality in education is one of the trickiest games in town. The problems appear in different contexts: they bother faculty committees and individual students in the endless efforts to define good teaching and to say who are the better—and the inadequate—teachers; they disturb deans, college presidents, and trustees who want to uplift weak academic departments and to maintain the strength of the better departments; and they confuse high school seniors and their counsellors in the search for colleges that are best suited to their needs. The ingredients of quality include some obvious features and some that are not so obvious. Faculty skills (both in subject-matter expertise and the ability to transmit their skills to students) appear in most discussions of educational quality. There are also elements of faculty size and accessibility to the students. Sometimes these features are described as the faculty-student ratio and sometimes as faculty interest in teaching. Some physical commodities add to quality education: laboratories, libraries, computers, and classroom facilities of appropriate size and convenience, with the equipment and collections that are adequate for the numbers of students at hand and their needs for special or sophisticated experiences (i.e., enough books or equipment of the right kinds for the training involved).

Not all ingredients of quality education can be ordered up and served by college administrators. Students themselves add much to one another's education. From one perspective, professors are only the organizers of materials and the intellectual cheerleaders who drum up enthusiasm for their fields. In the better schools, much learning and insight (about academic subjects as well as life in general) comes in student lounges and dormitory rooms. A good school is made better by the quality of students it attracts; they bring important experiences from their previous lives, transmit detailed information, and produce an appreciation of academic and other cultural pursuits. Institutional prestige is an element—and not only a reflection—of educational quality. Prestige helps attract good students (and well-trained faculty), and it thereby reinforces the other features (renown of the faculty or success of the alumni) that developed prestige in the first instance.

Diversity has something to do with good education. The diversity of faculty is subject to the control of a college administration by its efforts to recruit well-trained talent across a wide range of the academic disciplines. Diversity also helps if it appears in the student body and the cultural stimuli off-campus: concerts, museums, and theaters. A university located in a large metropolitan area offers the most cosmopolitan setting for its students. Even the small school in the hinterland can import some of this culture, however, by way of visiting artists, well-stocked reading rooms, film series, and programs that offer students the opportunity to spend a period of time in a wholly different setting (e.g., "junior year abroad," or "summer at the United Nations").

Many assessments of quality in education find that "it depends on the student's needs." What is quality for one student may be a detour for another. A top-rated mathematics department does not offer any direct assistance to a major in history. A freshman program designed to introduce a wide range of humanistic studies may bore or distract the committed engineer. On the other hand, the humanities program may offer a richer perspective to the student who chose engineering only because his or her high school could not arouse an interest in arts or letters. The simple matter of an institution's size may cause differences in its worth depending on the students' emotional needs. For some, the large university offers anonymity and tolerance so they can "do their thing." Others crave close personal relationships with members of the faculty; for them, the large university offers a poor substitute for the intimacy of a small college. If there is less privacy in the small school, there is also more chance for the individual to achieve some notice.

There are great differences in evaluations of graduate training and various forms of undergraduate education. Junior colleges and state colleges recruit students from different backgrounds than state universities and prestigious private institutions.[4] Student interests, preparation, and needs differ among these institutions. Where some colleges should be judged on their capacity to arouse students' intellectual interests or to provide marketable vocational skills, others should be judged on their provision of the most advanced and specialized faculty expertise.

Some efforts have specified criteria for various kinds of education and have ranked institutions. One of the most highly regarded deals with graduate education; it relies on professors' ranking of each other's universities. In 1964 and 1969 the American Council on Education asked a sample of faculty members to judge the "quality of graduate faculty" in their field of study at each university that offered doctoral-level work. The respondents included senior scholars, department chairpersons, and junior scholars. They were asked to rate each university according to their assessment of its graduate faculty as being "distinguished," "strong," "good," "adequate," "marginal," or "not sufficient for doctoral training." In each case, the respondents judged only the performance of other universities in their own field. That is, historians judged the quality of history faculties, and economists judged the quality of economics faculties.

There are advantages and disadvantages to a ranking of institutions on the basis of their faculties' reputation among other faculty members. The primary advantages are that the members of each field know the most about their colleagues at other institutions, they read their articles and books, and come to know one another through contacts at professional meetings. Presumably, judgments are made not on the basis of friendship, but on the basis of criteria of expertise that professionals take seriously. Also, the judgments are summary in nature; they represent each respondent's overall evaluation of separate features that make for faculty skill. The primary disadvantage is that a reputational assessment emphasizes the highly visible features of research and publication. It does not provide an independent check on the faculty members' accessibility to students, their classroom skills, or the spill-over of their talents to undergraduate education. In order to infer general institutional quality from the findings of this report, it is necessary to make some assumptions about the ways that faculty reputation may affect other segments of the educational process: by infusing into their own teaching the enthusiasm and advanced knowl-edge that comes from a career of research and writing; by recruiting skilled younger members to the faculty; and by attracting graduate students who may serve as teaching assistants in undergraduate courses.

By looking at the rankings of various institutions in the latest findings of the American Council on Education, it is possible to identify the most prominent universities in the country and to note the place in the elite that is held by private and public institutions. Table 4-1 shows the institutions ranked "distinguished" or "strong" by at least 50 percent of the respondents in at least two fields and the number of fields in which the institution achieved this distinction.[5]

The rankings of graduate faculties show the strength of three state universities and the continuing standing of prestigious private institu-tions. The University of California at Berkeley leads all other schools in the breadth of disciplines where it enjoys high quality ratings. Over half of the respondents judged its faculty "distinguished" or "strong" in 34 out of 36 of the fields considered in the study. Harvard is a distinct second, with this standing in 28 of the fields. As the opening paragraph of this chapter suggests, Harvard, Yale, and Princeton continue to rank high in prestige; they are all in the top group of eight universities. However, they are joined by two private universities from the Midwest and Pacific Coast (Chicago and Stanford) as well as by the state universities of Wisconsin and Michigan. Other state universities that rank high in at least five departments are Illinois, UCLA, and Minnesota. Six others have from two to four of their departments in the "distinguished" or "strong" categories.

Table 4-1   Universities Having at Least Two of Their Departments Rated "Distinguished" or "Strong" by a Majority of Academic Judges, 1969

University	Number of departments rated "distinguished" or "strong"
*University of California (Berkeley)	34
Harvard University	28
Yale University	23
Stanford University	22
*University of Wisconsin	21
*University of Michigan	19
University of Chicago	18
Princeton University	17
Columbia University	14
Massachusetts Institute of Technology	14
Cornell University	13
California Institute of Technology	12
*University of Illinois	10
*University of California (Los Angeles)	9
University of Pennsylvania	9
*University of Minnesota	6
John Hopkins University	5
University of Rochester	4
*University of Texas	4
*University of Washington	4
*University of North Carolina	3
Bryn Mawr College	2
Duke University	2
*Indiana University	2
New York University	2
Northwestern University	2
*Ohio State University	2
*Purdue University	2

Source: Derived from Kenneth D. Roose and Charles J. Andersen, *A Rating of Graduate Programs* (Washington: American Council on Education, 1970).
    *State universities.

ECONOMIC AND SOCIAL PAYOFFS FROM
HIGHER EDUCATION

In order to assess state activities in higher education it is necessary to look beyond sheer numbers of students enrolled, investments in bricks, mortar, faculty degrees and salaries, and even beyond educators' assessments of the outstanding institutions. Higher education offers some payoffs to state economies and cultures; it differs from other services in the outer limits that are expected from its benefits. State institutions do not invest billions of dollars simply to provide students with several years of maturation and a diploma. Higher education is the states' investment in their own economic growth and cultural enrichment. Expenditures should produce benefits across a wide range of activities. Many good things should result. They will come as the result of private as well as of public higher education. Because of the increasing state role, however, these benefits will increasingly reflect the contribution of state governments.

The payoffs of higher education include some readily measured benefits that go directly to the graduates and numerous benefits that go to society at large. Most of the social benefits are difficult to measure in any precise terms, but—to the extent that they actually do flow from higher education—they represent some of the most impressive payoffs of any service provided by state governments.

Chief among the personal benefits of higher education is the improved economic position of the alumnus. Higher education means higher earnings. Some of these benefits accrue to the student who takes advantage of *some* education beyond high school. For the student who remains in college long enough to earn a bachelor's degree there are even greater benefits. Likewise, the student who acquires some postgraduate training can expect higher earnings than the baccalaurate. One study finds that male college graduates had median incomes that were 34 percent above those of high school graduates. The differences do not merely reflect higher first job salaries for college graduates. The income differentials associated with education increase with age: for persons with 5 or more years of college, the median income at ages 30–34 is 33 percent higher than for persons who graduated only from high school; the differential increases to 55 percent at ages 35-44, and to 69 percent at ages 45-54.[6]

To be sure, the difference in income between college and noncollege persons is traceable to more factors than the college experience itself. There are differences in ability among adolescents that lead some to college and others to stop their education after high school. These same differences in ability affect their earning potential in later years. What portion of the later differentials in earning reflect the college experience? Some research into the subject indicates that about 25 percent of the differences reflect innate ability, with 75 percent of the differences left to be explained by the training received in higher education. Even making the adjustment for ability differences, there remains a considerable individual payoff from a college education. One study of college educated males in California found that lifetime additional incomes traceable to the college experience amounted to $89,000. This figure is given in terms of 1965 dollars and can be adjusted upward to account for anticipated inflation over the graduates' lifetimes. For those who attend college but do not graduate, the lifetime additional income is calculated at $20,400.[7]

The graduates and their immediate families are primary beneficiaries of income differentials that are associated with a college education. The society at large is a secondary beneficiary. Increased earnings reflect the increased value of graduates' labor. Presumably, their work has more economic and social utility than the work of high school graduates. Also, their greater income produces more tax revenues and thus makes a greater contribution to the whole range of public services supported by national, state, and local governments. The study of California males' calculated increased Federal taxes paid over a lifetime by college graduates would be $15,900 (in 1965 dollars), while the increased Federal taxes paid over a lifetime by those with some college would be $3,700.[8]

Some benefits from higher education result from the aggregation of scientific and literary talent in colleges and universities and the opportunities for the faculty and the community to profit from one another. Professors and their advanced students add to the pool of talent available to industry, government, and the local culture. Professors moonlight in the employ of industry and government. Prominent signs of faculty consulting appear in the industrial research facilities on the outskirts of Boston, Chapel Hill–Durham–Raleigh, and the San Francisco Bay area. Relationships between the state and the University of Wisconsin date to the administration of Robert M.

LaFollette in 1901–1906. The short distance between the campus and the capitol plays some part in the ties, but so does a feeling of mutual respect and dependence that is labeled the "Wisconsin idea."

Several states are trying to increase the economic and social payoffs of higher education by upgrading urban institutions. They tailor undergraduate education to urban work and living patterns and offer research inputs to the city's industry, commerce, and government. Classes run from early morning through the evening, libraries remain open 24 hours a day, storefront classrooms appear in ghetto areas away from the main campus, and schools of business and public administration make a special effort to train managers for local business and government. Examples are Wayne State University; University of California, Los Angeles; University of Massachusetts—Boston; University of Wisconsin—Milwaukee; University of Illinois at Chicago Circle; Georgia State University (Atlanta); the Universities of Missouri at Kansas City and St. Louis; Louisiana State University—New Orleans; the University of Colorado at Denver; and Cleveland State University. Florida and Alabama have sought to enhance their economies through institutions that were created to serve the space communities around Cape Kennedy and Huntsville. The universities of Michigan, Georgia, and North Carolina—among others—have improved their local economies—and have provided consulting opportunities for their faculties—by acquiring land and recruiting the research laboratories of private industry and Federal agencies.

An increasing number of universities operate programs to train public administrators. A 1974 survey by the National Association of Schools of Public Affairs and Administration reported about 101 programs with total graduate enrollments exceeding 13,000. Many students in these programs are already working in junior- or middle-management positions. In this way the institutions of higher education strengthen the decision-making procedures of the governments that support them. At least in a few instances known to the author, university-trained budget officers have used their improved skills to trim the financial requests made by their alma maters. In 1969–1970, 22 institutions (17 of them state supported) operated state and local government internship programs in conjunction with the American Political Science Association. Through this program, graduate students interrupted their education for full-time work experience in state or local governments. For some of the graduates, the experience will provide a clearer understanding of state and local government and will aid their own academic careers as political scientists. For others, however, the internship will be the first step toward a career in state or local administration.

Higher education provides special opportunities for the children of poor families and especially for the members of ethnic, racial, and religious minorities. Higher education is the "way out" or the "ticket to success" for those who would otherwise enter adulthood from a noncompetitive cultural background. Higher education provides not only economic opportunity but also the first taste of individual freedom. Compared to other sectors of the society, the college campus is relatively free from minority group stereotypes that keep individuals from maximizing their potential. A generation ago it was the Jews who found their best chance for individual success in college. More recently it is blacks and Latin Americans who find higher education to be the best route out of a background marked by discrimination. From 1964 to 1974, blacks increased their proportions from 5 to 9 percent of enrollments in higher education.

One of the complex issues in public higher education concerns the distributions of benefits from higher education and the distributions of its costs among state residents. "Who gets the education?" and "Who pays the bills?" are the important questions. Some policy makers feel that low-income people are paying more than the average cost for higher education, yet are receiving less than the average benefits.[9] This happens, presumably, because the tax systems that support higher education are regressive, while students from middle- and upper-income families take most advantage of its opportunities. To deal with these charges it is necessary to consider what kinds of taxes actually support public higher education and what kinds of students actually take advantage of higher education. To the extent that a state income tax provides the major support, then middle-and upper-income residents will pay more of the cost than where a sales tax carries the burden. It also depends on the mix of educational opportunities in a state and how convenient they are to centers of population. To the extent that low-income families live within easy commuting distance of junior colleges, vocational schools, or state colleges, there will be a higher incidence of lower-income beneficiaries. Conditions also vary with the percentage of educational costs that are passed to the students in the form of tuition and fees. The schools used mostly by low-income students (i.e., state colleges, junior colleges, and vocational schools) charge lower tuition in some states than the schools used mostly by the middle- and upper-income residents (i.e., the state university). Some states are more generous than others in scholarships, loans, and other financial aids. A few studies of higher education make a careful assessment of "Who pays the bills?" and "Who gets the benefits?" One study of California and Wisconsin credited Wisconsin with a more equitable distribution of costs and benefits. This is because Wisconsin's tax system is more progressive in imposing its highest rates on the upper-income classes, and because Wisconsin gave a substantially larger subsidy to students at the state colleges than to students at the university. Generally speaking, state college students are more likely to come from lower-income families than do university students.[10] And state college students in Wisconsin paid less of their education's full cost in tuition than did students at the University of Wisconsin.

State policy makers recognize the benefits that come from higher education. They show this not only in their willingness to vote increasing appropriations, but also in their responses to the questions of social scientists. Governors and legislators perceive that voters place a high value on educational opportunities for their children. Despite flurries of public sniping at the "ivory towers," policy makers support efforts to attract and retain high quality faculty members and to offer good salaries as the prime attractions. In many cases they have been willing to engage in interstate competition for a prestige system of higher education.[11] New York's "hundred-thousand dollar" professorial chairs for distinguished academicians like Marshall McLuhan and Arthur Schlesinger, Jr. were prominent entries in this competition. However, many legislators feel that faculty members do not work hard enough at teaching, have an easy life, or spend too much time on their own work (for which they receive additional compensation).

State officials are warm in their support of educational institutions that offer multiple payoffs. Historically, the favored schools were colleges of agriculture that trained farmers and produced research findings to increase farm productivity and the farmer's income. More recently, urban institutions have received special appropriations; not only because they offer educational services to a large market of available students (and without a high investment in dormitories), but also because they tout research and service programs for urban industry and the urban crisis.

Junior colleges are popular with legislators and budget makers. They are relatively inexpensive (almost all their funds go to teaching with virtually nothing for research) and serve a variety of needs. For the student interested in further academic training, they provide the first 2 years of a liberal arts education. They offer vocational training for the recent high school graduate, plus adult education and retraining for the community's elders. They provide educational opportunities for low-income students who cannot afford to leave home or who suffered the deprivations of poor elementary and secondary education. For many students they ease the transition between high school and higher education. An official in Kentucky expressed some beliefs that are shared widely among state legislators:

> They permit a greater number of children who are not financially able to leave their homes and live at a regional university to at least try college, to determine whether or not they're capable of doing college work and capable of going ahead. I think children who do well in community colleges probably can obtain financial aid to finish their college training, where these same children who had not been tested and tried at the community college level might never make it to college.[12]

In terms of enrollments added and institutions opened during the last few years, junior colleges are the most rapidly growing segment of higher education. In Florida and California, over 50 percent of the undergraduates are enrolled in 2-year institutions; in eight other states 30 percent or more are in 2-year institutions.[13] Almost all of the education thought of as "junior college" is financed by state or local governments. A study done in 1973 found that 76 percent of the institutions were public and 95 percent of the enrollments were in public colleges.

Some benefits from higher education are not primarily economic in nature. Graduates are more likely to support diverse and sophisticated art, music, and literature. Studies of voting behavior and public opinion show that college graduates take part in public affairs more than high school graduates. They are more tolerant of minority ethnic, religious, and racial groups and of minority viewpoints about public policy. The active, informed, and tolerant citizen that is assumed by theories of democratic government is likely to be a college graduate. Studies of several recent Presidential elections discovered sharp differences in voting participation between college and noncollege respondents. Women from outside the South with a college education voted at twice the rate of their counterparts with only a grade school education. Among Southern women, the college group voted more than six times the rate of women with a grade school education.[14] On opinion questions, college-educated persons show themselves more willing to accept taxation in order to pay for "important things that need to be done" and more likely to hedge their answers with a response that "it depends."[15] College-educated respondents are most likely to provide accurate answers to questions of fact dealing with political candidates or governmental programs. The following responses to survey questions suggest that college graduates are more tolerant of science and technology and have more sophisticated attitudes about their role in society.[16]

Attitude	Percent agreeing "strongly" or "somewhat"	
	Alumni	General population
Scientific research is causing the world to change too fast	26	54
Because the experts have so much power in our society, ordinary people don't have much of a say in things	38	72

The information and attitudes of college-educated persons reflect an interest in—and tolerance for—a wide range of opinions and perspectives. Undoubtedly, some of their information and perspective predates their collegiate experience. As in the case of income differentials, some of the differences between college and noncollege persons reflect innate characteristics of precollegiate experience. Yet existing differences are reinforced by college. There is some evidence that political perspectives widen during the college years.[17] Education should also work its influence after the college years by making graduates receptive to a wider range of cultural stimuli than are perceived by noncollege persons. One study finds that recent college graduates perceive themselves as being more liberal than their parents. Of the respondents, 40 percent identified their parents as having a liberal orientation and 52 percent claimed one for themselves.[18]

College may work its influence on succeeding generations through the child training provided by educated parents. Female graduates do not profit economically as much as males from higher education.[19] While they are home with the kiddies, however, they can provide them with a richer perspective on the world than is made available to the children of noncollege women. It is partly through the influence of well-educated parents that their teen-age children acquire the intellectual breadth and capacity that are reinforced by their own education in later years.

Colleges also provide a medium for changing a culture's values and practices. New ideas catch on most rapidly on the campus. The thousands of students who faced arrest and physical violence in the South during the sit-in and voter registration years of the early 1960s translated their views into political action. College people speeded the general liberalization of racial policies as manifest in civil rights legislation and administrative rulings for voting, public accommodations, housing, and jobs. The entrance of recent graduates into teaching, health, and welfare occupations shakes up bureaucracies and makes them receptive to innovative programs. The growing field of legal aid for the poor relies on recent law school graduates. Police departments in several cities want to improve their image and their service by recruiting college graduates. When the military faced resistance to its ROTC programs on the more prestigious campuses, it asked the unhappy students if they really want to close off the flow of well-educated, liberal graduates into the officer corps.

Some of the reaction against higher education testifies to its influence on social change. We cannot say with certainty what will happen as the present generation of students matures into adults and competes for positions in the economy and government. The commotions surrounding war, drugs, and sex may change our society in small or large dimensions. We also cannot say what part of students' attitudes results from the experience of higher education, and what part comes from national and international events that transpire far beyond the control of university faculty and administrators. Faculty members may have little to do with producing the values that disturb some politicians, voters, and parents. Nonetheless, when politicians take on the local university and say that "education is too important to be left entirely to the educators," we know that "ivory tower" is no longer an apt analogy.

NOTES

1 Unless otherwise indicated the data on finance, enrollments, institutions, and faculty in this chapter come from *Compendium of State Government Finances, 1974* (Washington: U.S. Government Printing Office, 1975); *Statistical Abstract of the United States, 1975* (Washington: U.S. Government Printing Office, 1975); *A Fact Book on Higher Education* (Washington: American Council on Education, 1969); *Budget of the United States: Special Analysis, Fiscal Year 1977* (Washington: U.S. Government Printing Office, 1976); *Book of the States, 1974–75* (Lexington, Council of State Governments, 1974).

2 See Philip G. Altbach, *Student Politics in America: A Historical Analysis* (New York: McGraw-Hill, 1974).

3 M. M. Chambers, "Appropriations of State Tax Funds for Operating Expenses of Higher Education, 1970–1971" (Washington: Office of Institutional Research, National Association of State Universities and Land-Grant Colleges, 1970).

4 See E. Alden Dunham, *Colleges of the Forgotten Americans: A Profile of State Colleges and Regional Universities* (New York: McGraw-Hill, 1969); and The Carnegie Commission on Higher Education, *The Open-Door Colleges: Policies for Community Colleges* (New York: McGraw—Hill, 1970).

5 The American Council on Education shies away from university-wide rankings. This reanalysis of its findings is offered with the caveat that it pertains to a limited range of the elements to be considered in judging the performance of universities—especially with respect to the quality of their undergraduate education. See

Kenneth D. Roose and Charles J. Andersen, *A Rating of Graduate Programs* (Washington: American Council on Education, 1970).

6 W. Lee Hansen and Burton A. Weisbrod, *Benefits, Costs, and Finance of Public Higher Education* (Chicago: Markham, 1969), pp. 18–19.

7 Hansen and Weisbrod, p. 19–27.

8 Hansen and Weisbrod, pp. 22, 27. These data result after controlling for the portion of increased earnings and taxes that are traceable to innate ability instead of the collegiate experience.

9 See Hansen and Weisbrod. For contrasting views see Ira Sharkansky, "Communication," *The Journal of Human Resources*, 5 (Spring 1970), pp. 230–236; and Joseph A. Pechman, "The Distributional Effects of Public Higher Education in California," *The Journal of Human Resources*, 5 (Summer 1970), pp. 361–370.

10 W. Lee Hansen, "Income Redistribution Effects of Higher Education," a paper presented at the annual meeting of the American Economic Association, 1969, New York. This study reflects conditions prior to the merger in Wisconsin of the university and the state-college systems.

11 Heinz Eulau and Harold Quinley, *State Officials and Higher Education: A Survey of the Opinions and Expectations of Policy Makers in Nine States* (New York: McGraw-Hill, 1970), p. 102.

12 Eulau and Quinley, p. 120.

13 *The Open-Door Colleges*, p. 14.

14 Angus Campbell et al., *The American Voter* (New York: Wiley, 1960), p. 495.

15 V. O. Key, *Public Opinion and American Democracy* (New York: Knopf, 1961), pp. 337–339.

16 Joe L. Spaeth and Andrew M. Greeley, *Recent Alumni and Higher Education: A Survey of College Graduates* (New York: McGraw-Hill, 1970), p. 26.

17 Theodore M. Newcomb, *Personality and Social Change* (New York: Dryden, 1943).

18 Spaeth and Greeley, p. 100.

19 Hansen and Weisbrod, p. 22.

Chapter 5

States in the Federal System

The states are not alone. They all draw sizable funds from the United States Treasury, and almost all state agencies receive some directives from the national government. Extensive Federal aid to state and local governments came with the Depression. It grew from $232 million in 1932 to $945 million in 1940, and it has continued growing to $60.5 billion in 1977.

Even for a partisan of the states, it is necessary to concede that the national government helps a great deal. Yet portions of the Federal help are arbitrary in their design and misallocated in their administration; in some programs, Federal agencies generate major problems for state officials and citizens. It is easy to exaggerate the role of the national government. One of the great ironies in Federal-state relations is that both ultraliberal critics of the state governments and ultraconservative advocates of states rights argue that Washington has more control over the states than is actually the case. For the liberal, the national government is responsible for much of what is good about the states. For the conservative, the national government chokes any state efforts at individuality or creativity. Both partisans are wrong. There is much slippage in Washington's control over the grants-in-aid programs. State officials have important influence over the programs' design and implementation. Even in the programs with reputations for rigid central control, the states have shown creative efforts in their own policies.

Virtually all major Federal grants-in-aid borrowed heavily from the experiments of state governments. Numerous state universities antedate Federal acts for the support of land-grant colleges; there was an extensive system of limited access highways before the Interstate and Defense Highway Act; the Office of Economic Opportunity took important cues from projects funded by the Ford Foundation in conjunction with New York and North Carolina; 10 states provided old-age pensions by 1930—5 years before Old Age Assistance came with the United States Social Security Act.[1]

One critic of Federal programs writes that they emphasize glamorous additions to basic programs funded with state money, and that the Federal contributions are puffed up in their importance by public relations.

> Some . . . have had the impression that highways are built mostly with Federal dollars. This impression may be, in part, the result of effective public relations. Most states take it for granted that the taxpayers, seeing grading and paving machines and new roads, assume the state gasoline tax is at work. But the Federal government doesn't risk such assumptions. For every road built or improved, the state or the contractor must erect a sign proclaiming "Your Highway Taxes at Work" in eight-inch block letters, with the amounts of the funds from each government, and other information as required by Act of Congress . . . and spelled out by almost ten pages of guidelines. It is a small matter, but worth noting, that the signs applauding the work must be 6 feet by 13 feet when the Federal funds are 90 percent . . . but only 4 feet by 8 feet when the Federal funds are 50 percent of the costs. . . . All state schools must comply with the sign requirements, and even a little church college has to put the congregations in the back pews and post a red, white, and blue sign if it receives Federal money under the Higher Education Facilities Act. . . . It is proper to remember, however, for all the advantages brought by the extras, the train was put on the track in the first place by the states, and continues to be moved by state fuel and engineers.[2]

Some states play their own public relations game with the Federally required signs. When the University of Georgia put the necessary red, white, and blue signs outside the projects being supported with Federal money, it attached a small sign: "This sign imposed on the State of Georgia by requirements of the U.S. Department of Health, Education, and Welfare."

The Federal programs are charged with more serious deficiencies than upstaging the states in public relations. A whole set of problems results from the variety of different programs with overlapping target groups. Without any effective means of coordination, state officials face certain frustration in their efforts to develop programs that cut across the boundaries of different Federal activities. Related programs are supported by different agencies of the same Cabinet Department or by agencies in different Cabinet Departments. The President's budget for 1977 lists education funds amounting to $18.2 billion divided among the activities of all 11 Cabinet Departments, the Library of Congress, 2 units in the Executive Office of the President, and 11 independent offices. The Federal government sponsors coordinating mechanisms at the levels of state governments and metropolitan areas, and it has established coordinating committees for the Federal departments and agencies in Washington and regional offices. Yet there remain serious problems of Federal units that seem bent on avoiding any compromise of their own missions for the sake of coordination and a surplus of coordinating mechanisms that beg for coordination among themselves. The coordinators need a coordinator.

> If the community-level coordinating structures . . . are left to the sponsorship of individual Federal agencies, it is doubtful that any of them will prove effective in knitting together in the communities the programs of many Federal agencies. . . .
>
> The facts of bureaucratic life are that no Cabinet department has ever been able to act effectively, for long, as a central coordinator of other departments of equal rank that are its competitors for authority and funds. Nor does coordination spring readily from the mutual adjustment of Cabinet-level equals within the Federal hierarchy.[3]

Federal programs also impose arbitrary procedures on state recipients and evade the stickiest issues in the activities they help to finance. Public assistance programs are notorious for the inequities between state welfare programs that they encourage, and the highway programs leave the states to absorb the inevitable tensions produced by route selection and the uprooting of business and population.

FEDERAL AID AND STATE AUTONOMY

There is some truth to the notion of an increasing role for national government in state affairs. Since the Depression, Federal aid has provided a gradually increasing share of state funds, as shown in Table 5-1. Federal aid to state and local governments in 1977 was spread over more than 1,000 separate programs that ranged from agriculture to veterans affairs. Every Cabinet Department offers some money to states or communities. Most programs and funds come from Health, Education and Welfare; Housing and Urban Development; and Transportation. However, even the Defense and State Departments support activities such as the National Guard and international cultural activities. But despite the grants-in-aids, Federal expenditures for other domestic activities have not kept pace with state efforts. When we view the Federal government's support for all domestic programs in relation to that of state and local governments, we find that since World War II the greatest increase has been in the states' share. (See pp. 55-59.) Surely these figures reflect continuing vitality in state governments.

Any inquiry into the accomplishments, problems, and opportunities of state governments must recognize that they are not solely responsible for each failure or success. They are enmeshed in numerous and complex relationships with the national government on one side and with their local governments on the other side. Federal relationships offer money and technical assistance to state governments and impose program requirements and obligations that narrow the range in which state officials can design their own activities. There are hardly any state programs of importance that are free from the resources or the demands of other government authorities. Some of what is wrong or right with state programs should properly be blamed or credited to other governments.

To some extent, this chapter covers ground mapped earlier. It reminds us to temper our evaluation of state governments by recognizing their dependence on other actors. Yet it also shows how state governments acquire substantial freedom from the program requirements that come with Federal aids. It examines some general features of relation-

Table 5-1 Federal Role in State Finances, 1902–1974

	States' total general revenue from state sources (× 1,000,000)	State revenue from Federal government (× 1,000,000)	Federal aid as a % of state revenue
1974	$89,157	$31,632	35.5
1969	49,537	16,907	34.1
1965	30,610	9,874	32.2
1954	12,417	2,668	21.4
1950	8,839	2,275	25.7
1946	5,419	802	14.7
1940	3,657	667	18.2
1936	2,914	719	24.6
1932	2,156	222	10.2
1922	1,128	99	8.7
1913	360	6	1.6
1902	183	3	1.6

Sources: U.S. Bureau of the Census, *Historical Statistics of Governmental Finances and Employment; Census of Governments, 1967* (Washington: GPO, 1969); and U.S. Bureau of the Census, *State Government Finances, 1969 and 1974* (Washington: GPO, 1975).

ships between state and national governments, and it looks closely at three areas where the national government appears dominant: transportation, welfare, and race. In transportation and welfare the Federal dominance seems to accompany massive amounts of intergovernmental aid; in race it comes with decisions of the Federal courts, the Congress, and the Administration in default of sufficient prior action by state authorities. In each of these fields, however, much discretion is left in the hands of state authorities, and state officials use their opportunities in distinctive and commendable ways.

Grants-in-aid are the single most prominent feature of Federal relations with state and local governments. In 1977 they amounted to 85 percent of all Federal aids. Each Federal grant supports a specific state or local program; they do not provide general support of state activities. They typically require that recipient agencies submit detailed applications for the funds, provide some of their own resources to support the aided activities, and administer the program according to prescribed standards. The "program" nature of Federal grants and the requirements that come along with the money are frequent sources of conflict between Federal and state officials. It is said that Federal carrots lead recipients to undertake activities that are not in their own best interest, and that Federal requirements are frequently inconsistent with the states' social or economic problems.

The allegations about Federal controls are more easily stated than demonstrated. In order to weigh the capacity of Federal agencies to alter the practices of state agencies, it is necessary to take account of several features that may affect their influence over state programs:

1   The extent to which potential state recipients actually make use of the resources that are offered

2   The extent to which recipients seek to evade the requirements of an intergovernmental program that are designed to stimulate changes in existing policies

3   The extent to which the Federal grantor declines to monitor the program performance of the recipient or declines to enforce those requirements that are designed to provoke changes in the recipients' policies

4   The routinization of procedures followed by both the grantor and the recipient which smother the policy control potential of an intergovernmental program in its own standard operating procedures

1.   The appeal of intergovernmental programs for potential recipients.   Before an intergovernmental program can possibly have an impact on a recipient, the program must be adopted. If a program is not adopted, none of the policy changes desired by the granting agencies occur. Most Federal programs seem to be used heavily. They certainly move a lot of resources from higher to lower jurisdictions. Yet there are many questions that remain unanswered about the *extent* of each program's use.

In the case of one set of intergovernmental programs—those funded by the U.S. Office of Economic Opportunity—there is some evidence that *they were adopted most rapidly where they were needed the least.* One study found that states with well-established and generous programs in the fields of welfare, health, and education were the most likely to make early use of OEO programs.[4] Features of the states' economies, popular participation in politics, party competition, and the equity of urban-rural apportionment in the state legislatures had relatively little to do with the adoption of antipoverty programs. Established programs in functionally related areas were most important. These findings suggest the workings of incremental policy making in the adoption of new Federal programs. Where new programs represent little departure from established activities, they are most readily adopted. Where the programs threaten an innovation in state programs, however, they may come slowly and at lower-than-average levels of use into the states' activities.

Similar evidence comes from studies into the political characteristics of cities that adopt antipoverty programs. Those cities which historically made the greatest use of programs that distributed material benefits to the voters made the greatest use of the new programs. Two cities with strong political machines (Chicago and Philadelphia) took greater immediate advantage of the new programs than did two cities without strong political machines (Los Angeles and New York). The evidence is only sketchy, but it does suggest the importance of established procedures and the inclination to adopt programs that do not threaten a major departure from current practices.

> Since machines were historically dependent on the efficient payment of material benefits to their various supporters, it is not surprising to find that greater organizational strength increases the mayor's ability to obtain and distribute poverty funds. By contrast, the far greater concern of reform movements for "democracy" and "honesty" in political processes and structures, as opposed to the distribution of material outputs, explain the less effective distribution of funds by poverty agencies in cities with strong reform traditions.[5]

2. and 3. Pressures on the recipients and the grantor that minimize central control of intergovernmental programs. Several elements tempt recipient agencies to maximize their freedom from the grantor's concern with policy control and tempt the granting agencies to permit that freedom. These include the localistic tendencies in the Federal culture of the United States and the numerous political mechanisms that give state and local agencies some measure of control over their nominal superiors. Legislators, executives, and administrators at each level of government say it is a good thing for local and state officials to have maximum autonomy from outside controls.[6] These sentiments by themselves do not provide recipient agencies with the freedom they desire, but the recipients have other resources that support their appeals to Federal legislators and executives. Federal agencies are sensitive to the wishes of Congress and the White House about the overly strict control of intergovernmental programs.

At times, recipient agencies have resisted unwanted changes in their own programs, and granting agencies have been weak in promoting their policies. The record of state compliance with Federal regulations for unemployment and welfare programs during the early days of the New Deal was notorious for evasions on the part of state officials. According to one Federal agent sent to check on state administrators in Oklahoma, there was "thieving and favortism on all sides. I found that every Tom, Dick, and Harry in the state was getting relief whether they were unemployed or not." Federal officials prevailed upon Oklahoma's governor to dismiss some ineffective county administrators. But soon after the Federal official left the state, the governor appointed another group of his cronies to the program and blamed Washington for the earlier removals.[7] At the Federal level, there is some evidence that President Roosevelt ordered his subordinates to use the grants-in-aids in order to discipline recalcitrant politicians who had opposed his Administration. The following conversation recorded between the President and Vice President Garner indicates that patronage features of New Deal programs competed with their use in state policy control:

> Roosevelt: "Don't put anybody in and don't keep anyone that is working for Huey Long or his crowd! That is a hundred percent!"
>
> Garner: "That goes for everybody!"
>
> Roosevelt: "Everybody and every agency. Anybody working for Huey Long is not working for us."[8]

Many years after certain Federal programs have gone into effect, they have not obliterated existing inclinations in states and regions. Welfare programs provide a clear indication of this tendency. Average payments to recipients are generally lower than average in those states and regions that have a conservative orientation toward social services, while they are markedly higher than average in those states and regions with a progressive reputation.[9] The availability of Federal funds may have diminished what otherwise would have been larger differentials between progressive and conservative states. But the differentials remain large in size. To cite just one example, average monthly payments for recipients of Old Age Assistance in 1973 were $121 in Massachusetts and $57 in South Carolina. Moreover, Massachusetts' officials have paid their highest grants in the poorest counties of their state, while South Carolinians paid their highest grants in the wealthiest counties of their state.

   4. The routinization of procedures by grantors and recipients.   If a Federal program can upset the policy inclinations of recipient governments, that opportunity seems greatest in the first years of the program's operation. A new activity starts with a base of zero, and its first growth is financed and directed by Federal money. For many Federally aided programs, however, there is a base of existing policy in a similar state program. As we have already seen, this existing layer can shape the use that is made of the Federal money. As Federal programs mature, the granting agency might continue to monitor the recipients' policies. However, the organizational pressures on both the grantor and the recipient are in the direction of routinization.[10] Moreover, recipients have the protection of local political cultures and their ties to Congress and the Federal executive to protect their decision routines from outside interference.

   One case of routinized intergovernmental relations appeared in the public assistance programs created by the Social Security Act of 1935. A study of public assistance written in the early 1960s found that the controversy surrounding the programs was not matched by any concerted efforts to change the programs. Charges of widespread cheating, illegitimacy, and transfer of welfare status from one generation to the next were not reflected in any effort on the part of welfare officials to design, implement, or lobby for a major reform in their programs.[11] Some program features seemed to reinforce existing levels of poverty in certain states and regions. The Federal-state aid formulas gave a higher Federal percentage of the total cost of those states that offered their recipients lower-than-average welfare payments. As a state's payments to a recipient increased, the Federal government's share of the payment decreased. The program supported a minimum level of aid throughout the country and put the burden for increasing generosity on the states themselves. In the poorest states, which also had the highest incidence of welfare recipients, the formulas discouraged any-thing more than a subsistence level of aid. These Federal-state formulas were said to produce gross inequities in opportunities between North and South, the mass migrations of poor whites and blacks from South-ern rural to Northern urban areas, plus the whole range of social dis-locations that accompany the migrations.

> American public assistance policy has been stable for 30 years. This
> stability—or, from another point of view, sterility—is more readily
> traced to an absence of innovative proposals than to any consensus
> that the categorical assistance programs spelled out in the Social
> Security Act of 1935 have continuing validity. Stability is less a
> matter of widespread satisfaction with the program than it is the
> absence of an informed, influential group with a better idea.[12]

Some people had better ideas about public welfare since the enactment of the Social Security Act of 1935. The war on poverty with its myriad of education, employment, health, and political action programs was the first major effort at welfare reform. This did not come until 1964, however, and it occurred outside of the agencies charged with the public assistance programs. The United States Welfare Administration and state departments of welfare were given few if any important re-sponsibilities in the war on poverty. They had become so closely iden-tified with the unsatisfactory programs for the categories of aid (aged, blind, disabled, and families of dependent children) that they were seen as incapable of adopting to a more inclusive program against poverty. Since then, additional reforms have sought to standardize certain wel-fare programs with heavier doses of Federal aid and control. As we see below, however, these have yet to prove their capacity to undo prob-lems that had been reinforced by many years of inaction.

A second case of routinized intergovernmental relations appears in the Federal program to aid school districts "impacted" with population from military installations or industries doing business with the Federal government. This program began during World War II to aid those local governments whose school enrollments increased rapidly with the in-flux of Federally related personnel. Once the communities' populations at their new level, the added property taxes reflecting the new population could, presumably, handle any enrollments that were larger than the preimpact period. The program's rationale became more complex as more and more school districts received the children of Federally related personnel during the cold war. The program was justified partly because it funneled large sums of Federal money into the states, whereas a more general program of aid to education could not pass through a Congress that was sensitive to issues of racial integration and Federal aid to parochial schools. In 1977 the program to aid impacted areas continues. It is not helping local school districts over the first hump of a rapidly increased population. For most of the localities receiving aid, that hump occurred in the 1940s. The program no longer meets a need to provide some Federal relief for general school costs; that justification eroded with the passage of numerous Federal education programs in the 1950s and 1960s. The principal justification for the program to aid impacted areas appears to be its existence and its solid place in the policy-making routines of Federal and local agencies. Presidents Eisenhower, Kennedy, Johnson, Nixon, and Ford have urged its phasing out. But each time the favored local administrators and their allies in Congress resisted the change. Current spending is about $400 million annually. The program testifies to the tenure of an intergovernmental program. Moreover, by providing a base of Federal aid to thousands of school districts that is not tied to any carefully monitored effort to stimulate policy innovations, the impacted areas program may blunt pressures for more broadly based aid to education programs that would carry innovative stimuli.

REVENUE-SHARING: DOES IT PRODUCE MORE OR LESS CREATIVE POLICY?

Revenue-sharing is the most important innovation in the recent history of Federal aid. Since 1972 it has provided more than $6 billion per year, with two-thirds allocated directly to localities and one-third to state governments. Revenue-sharing differs from traditional grants-in-aid in its lack of strings or complex administrative procedures. States and localities receive the money without detailed applications. The formulas assign larger sums to states and localities with larger populations, higher incidences of poor residents, and higher rates in their own taxes. State governments have no program restrictions on their use of the funds; but they must not use the money in ways that discriminate among people on the basis of race, color, national origin, or sex, or to undercut wages paid for construction activities in their areas.

During 1972–1973, state governments reported that they used 70 percent of their revenue shares for education, much of it passed on to local school districts. Social services, transportation, and health each received between 3 and 7 percent of the total. Local governments face more restrictions on their use of revenue-sharing (they cannot use it to support the operating expenses of schools) and their reports show a wider distribution to more services: 35 percent to public safety; 20 percent to transportation; and 6 to 10 percent to environmental protection, general government, health, and recreation.

The enactment of revenue-sharing was preceded by extensive disputes about its impact. Would its lack of controls encourage creativity or waste? In actual practice, the result of $6 billion given to thousands of state and local agencies each year has produced its share of creative and wasteful responses. Most officials at all levels seem satisfied with the program and now look at it less as a creative experiment than as a substantial flow of funds that must continue. Soon after the revenue-sharing enactment, Washington reduced spending for other aid programs, thus forcing state and local governments to use their revenue shares for substitute funding more than would have been the case otherwise. About one-third of state revenue-sharing receipts went to new programs during the first 18 months of the program's operation. Other large sums have been used to meet demands in established programs, in order to defer or ease tax increases.[13]

The major theme of this book (the states are alive and well) puts us on the side of revenue-sharing that leaves important program discretions in the hands of state officials. Another theme, however (some states do offer backward programs), cautions that revenue-sharing is not the whole answer to states' revenue needs. There will remain sharp inequities between the programs offered to citizens of different states. Some of these (e.g., public assistance) are sufficiently out of step with preferred living conditions to invite a direct attack with Federal money and Federal standards. This means either closely monitored Federal aids to states with abnormally low welfare payments or the total replacement of the public assistance grants-in-aid with a welfare program that is administered by the Federal government. We return to the topic of revenue-sharing in Chapter 7, pp. 156–158.

STATE ACTIONS IN THREE "FEDERALLY DOMINATED" FIELDS: TRANSPORTATION, WELFARE, AND RACE

Despite the inhibitions to strict Federal control that lie in the relationships between Washington and the state capitals, there are some programs where the national government seems dominant. The supporter of state governments has the toughest arguments where Federal leadership seems to have come because the states have insufficient resources for the problems at hand, or because the states have been unwilling to change their own inadequate or insensitive policies. Yet even where these charges are made, there is important evidence about the responsiveness and the initiative of the states. This section considers state roles in transportation, welfare, and race.

TRANSPORTATION

For most Americans, the favored mode of transportation is the family auto. For governments, too, the auto is the most favored vehicle. Highways take the lion's share of national, state, and local transportation budgets. Federal transportation aids to state and local governments included $6.4 *billion* for highways in 1976, but only $1.5 *billion* for urban mass transit, $375 *million* for airports, and $19 *million* for railroads. State spending during the same year allocated $15.8 *billion* to highways and only $277 *million* to airports.

The Federal government is a leading partner in this most demanding of transportation modes. More than one-fourth of state highway expenditures in 1974 came initially from the Federal government. Highways are second only to welfare in the dependence of state programs on Federal money. The most heavily traveled interurban routes are Federally supported highways. Federal approval is required for those roads most wanted by the population and most important in current highway priorities. The U.S. Department of Transportation also provides leadership for highway-related ventures: highway beautification, upgrading of roadways for purposes of safety, and vehicle inspection.

A visible spin-off of Federal leadership is the extension of interstate standards to heavily traveled routes in state highway systems. Newer state roads have wide travel lanes and median strips, restricted access, and huge signs that give advance warning to exit ramps.

The Interstate Highway Program is one of the most visible and expensive grants-in-aid. Its supporters call it the greatest public works venture in the history of the world! Whether great or the greatest, the origins of the I-system came from the states themselves. The basic models were the Pennsylvania Turnpike, the Merritt Parkway and Wilbur Cross Highways in Connecticut, the Westchester Parkway System north of New York City, and the California Freeways. Each of these state systems was in operation during the 1940s.

Within the scope of all Federal highway programs, the state governments still have important options. In the aggregate of all Federal and state highway programs, the states provide more than 70 percent of the money and virtually all of the design, supervision of construction, and maintenance. Even though they may use a great deal of Federal money and live within Federal standards and approvals, the state departments of highways make the crucial decisions about route selection and road construction. The selection and development of highway routes are not simple administrative procedures. They trigger the most intense of political issues. Decisions involve economic growth or decay for individual communities and whole regions of a state. To choose one route or another between major cities will affect industrial development along the route that is chosen and may stifle development elsewhere. To grant or deny a community's demand for an exit ramp will determine whether it is given access to the economic boom that comes along with a major highway. Within cities, the highway can divide or put boundaries around residential communities. Construction of a new road may bring urban renewal together with the benefits and problems of family relocation, minority group relations, and the inflation of property values. That some highway departments deal with these issues better than others is evident from the differential rates of completion in the interstate system. Over the country as a whole, 83 percent of the allocated miles were in operation as of 1973. The ranges of completion went from 97 and 95 percent in Arkansas and Kansas to 46 and 64 percent in Hawaii and Louisiana.

A long-standing controversy in state highway policy concerns urban versus rural allocations of state funds. The rural emphasis of state aid highway budgets was one of the features said to be shaped by the rural domination of state legislatures.[14] Now rural domination of state politics has declined as a result of enforced reapportionments of state legislatures. Perhaps in response to reapportionment—or in response to a more basic awakening of interest in urban problems—an increasing portion of state highway funds was allocated to urban areas by state governments: from 29.9 percent in 1962 to 35.8 percent in 1967.[15] Some states showed greater progress than others in allocated highway money to their cities. The percentage of Georgia's highway aid going to urban areas went from 9.6 to 49.8. In Illinois, however, there was a small reversal: from 49.6 to 44.5 percent of the aid went to cities.

Numerous states have sought to expand the scope of their transportation policies beyond the traditional preoccupation with highways. By 1974, 25 states had created integrated departments of transportation, with an eye toward broadening the consideration of policy alternatives across the various modes of transportation. The major departure from highway construction has been in urban mass transit. The Federal government has provided important leadership and resources in this field, partly by allowing some of the Highway Trust Fund to be used for public transportation and partly via new grant-in-aid programs under the Urban Mass Transportation Administration. Although much policy making in this field relies on Federal-local relations, state governments have provided additional financing, either as grants from their general funds or as dedicated taxes. Massachusetts allocates a share of its cigarette tax and Colorado a part of its sales tax to mass transportation. Maryland's Department of Transportation provides bus and rail transportation in the Baltimore metropolitan area and helps to support the Washington Metro Rapid Rail.

No-fault insurance for automobile drivers represents an aspect of transportation policy where the process of state innovation and Federal response is in the works. Massachusetts was the first state to adopt a no-fault system in 1970. It differed from traditional auto insurance by promising benefits quickly to the victims of auto accidents, without lengthy and expensive procedures to determine who was at fault. By 1974 all of the state legislatures had considered the Massachusetts reform, and 19 states had adopted some version of it. Congress has also given serious consideration to establishing national standards for the no-fault system. This procedure is far from complete, as various enactments and proposals differ in important details and have provoked active debates about their advantages and disadvantages.

WELFARE

The Federal government appears to dominate the field of public welfare even more fully than transportation. As it is most commonly defined in this country, "welfare" means public assistance: aid to the aged; blind; permanently and totally disabled; aid to families of dependent children; medicaid; and general assistance. General assistance (sometimes called "relief") is a residual category that aids those persons who do not qualify for the other programs. All programs except general assistance are funded partially with Federal money and operate under Federal regulations. Each program emphasizes payments for indigents. Except for provisions to encourage the training and employment of the poor, they are support programs. Their chief purpose is to pay for subsistence and *not* to alter the recipients' skills, motivations, or employability. During 1974 the states spent $22.5 billion for public assistance, with $13.3 billion coming from the Federal government. No other major service of state or local governments relies to this extent (approximately 60 percent) on Federal funds.

It is unnecessary to say in this book what has been written so often: that public assistance programs have left much to be desired. The charges directed against them include:

1 Payment levels are not adequate to provide a decent standard of living.

2 Programs define eligible recipients in an arbitrary manner and fail to reach millions of near poor individuals.

3 Requirements impose harsh burdens on the recipients' personal lives, and they present economic incentives for promiscuity, illegitimacy, and continued unemployment.

4 There are sharp variations in program coverage and generosity from one state to another that produce inequalities among recipients, induce recipients to move from low-payment to high-payment jurisdictions, and thereby impose economic and social costs on the high-payment jurisdictions. For 1973, the highest and lowest payments, by state, were:

	High	Low
Dependent Children	$279.86 (N.Y.)	$52.22 (Miss.)
Aged	$170.79 (N.H.)	$50.12 (Miss.)
Blind	$172.07 (Alaska)	$66.83 (Miss.)
Disabled	$169.99 (Alaska)	$60.35 (La.)
General Assistance	$185.97 (Hawaii)	$12.48 (Ala.)

Many of these problems have come from the Federal legislation (the Social Security Act of 1935, as amended) that creates the basic standards for each program and provides the incentives that lead various states to high or low payment levels. Federal provisions have encouraged the low-income states (with lots of very poor residents) to offer the lowest welfare payments. At one time the Federal government provided 31/37 of the first $37 in benefits for Old Age Assistance. Above $31 the Federal contribution dropped to somewhere between 50 and 65 percent of the total, with the lower-income states getting the higher Federal percentage. However, the maximum Federal contribution was $37.50 per case. For states that paid the highest benefits the money came entirely from their own resources after that Federal maximum was reached. As these formulas worked in practice, low-income states received a higher percentage of their expenditures as a Federal grant when they offered low payments to their recipients. With lots of potential recipients and meager resources, many poor states did not exceed the benefit levels that received heavy Federal support. Mississippi, for example, received 83 percent Federal reimbursement for its low payments, while New York received only 50 percent reimbursement for its high payments.[16] The natural course of action for Mississippi and other low-incomes states was to offer the low payments, receive the top Federal dollar, and provoke welfare recipients to move elsewhere.

A new Federal-state welfare program went into operation in 1974 for the purpose of making grants and administration more uniform throughout the country. For aids to the blind, disabled, and aged, the Federal government offered a minimum payment. States could elect to increase this with their own funds and could choose either state or national administration of the programs. The provision for state supplementing will assure some variation between high and low benefits from one state to another. During the first year of Supplemental Security Income, for example, aged recipients in Massachusetts received an average $140.74 per month, while those in Mississippi received $70.07. Yet there has been an important shift in principle. Now the national government, rather than the states, will set the minimum standards of assistance and define uniform eligibility criteria. While states with more generous traditions of welfare are likely to continue offering higher-than-average grants, the gap between the states seems likely to diminish. Before the initiation of the new reform, Old Age Assistance averaged 2.2 times greater in Massachusetts than in Mississippi. In the first year of the new program, the gap was reduced to 2.0 times greater.

The Federal base and option for state supplements suggest that the poor will continue to be better off if they live in wealthy states. What is natural and what happens, however, is not always the same thing. Numerous states dig deep into their citizens' pockets to pay for welfare programs that are considerably more generous than could be expected on the basis of their own resources or the Federal provisions. Table 5-2 lists four states making payments to the families of dependent children or general assistance payments that require more than the average amount of strain. In the case of general assistance, the program standards and the funds come entirely out of state legislatures and local governments. As in other cases of poor states trying hard, it is not easy to determine how much time we should spend on the applause of the states and how much on the condemnation of the Federal government. For Mississippi, Alabama, and other states that offer the very lowest welfare payments, it is appropriate to ask how much is due to their own conservatism and poverty and how much to the provisions of the Federal statutes.

Other programs outside of public assistance or welfare payments fall into a wider conception of public welfare. Two of them account for major investments by national, state, and local governments: unemployment compensation and the mix of programs that Lyndon Johnson included in his war on poverty. In both cases, the Federal government provides important sources of funds and/or the prominent stimuli for program development, but states have room for their own activities.

Unemployment compensation operates almost entirely under state funds. However, the funds are extracted from state taxpayers with the irresistible prompting of Federal legislation. If ever the iron fist-velvet

Table 5-2 State Welfare Payments Ranking Higher than Expected on Basis of Economic Resources, 1973

	Ranking on:	
	Per capita income	Monthly grant aid to families of dependent children
Wisconsin	27	2 ($262.87)
Vermont	38	8 ($233.44)
New Hampshire	29	13 ($221.53)
		Monthly grant general assistance
Virginia	24	14 ($98.45)
Wisconsin	27	15 ($96.25)
Vermont	38	17 ($94.87)

Source: The Book of the States, 1974–1975 (Lexington, Ky.: The Council of State Governments, 1974).

glove analogy was appropriate for a Federal-state program, this is it. The program began in 1935 when the Federal government enacted a payroll tax to be paid by employers in each of the states. As each state set up a program of unemployment compensation to be funded with a similar payroll tax of its own, state employers would be excused from up to 90 percent of the Federal tax—depending on the level of the state program. The remaining 10 percent of the Federal tax would be made available to the states for the purpose of administering their employment program. All states enacted a program within 2 years. To do otherwise would deprive state employers of the Federal tax, and it would deprive state employees of the unemployment coverage.[17] However, numerous provisions of the program are left in the hands of state authorities. Some state-to-state differences are evident in average payments available to beneficiaries. The maximum weekly benefit allowed in Connecticut was $138 during 1973, while the maximum allowed in Mississippi was $49.

A whole series of new programs appeared on the welfare menu during the Johnson Administration. There were separate efforts in preschool, elementary, and secondary education for the poor; job training and placement; health care; and the development of political action in poor communities. They were to provide the means and the stimuli for the poor to leave their misery. To the generals and soldiers of the war on poverty, the established public assistance programs were inadequate at best or part of the enemy at worst. Minimum economic support was not enough. In Washington and in the states, the new programs were separated administratively from public assistance in order to free them from alien perspectives among those charged with the established welfare programs. Some new activities sought to improve the operation of existing programs. Government-supported "Outreach" began to seek out potential welfare recipients and inform them about their benefits. This helped to move state welfare expenditures upward at a rate 67 percent greater than total state expenditures during 1969-1973.

The states were not without their own opportunities in the war on poverty. State governments could make it easy or difficult for local governments and private organizations to avail themselves of the Federal opportunities, and the states themselves put more or less of their own money into the programs. States varied in the extent to which their residents and communities made use of the programs. The programs came fastest where they seemed to threaten the least departure from existing activities. It is ironic (given the perspectives of the reformers) that states with well-established traditional programs in the fields of education, health, and welfare (i.e., public assistance) offered the greatest welcome to the war on poverty.[18]

Some research in Massachusetts shows what a state can do with its own antipoverty programs. Massachusetts' total antipoverty effort in 1968 included the established public assistance payments, as well as programs to improve the health, job capabilities, housing, environment, and education of the poor and near-poor. The state government did a little better than the Federal government and much better than the localities in funding these programs. While the Federal government provided 11.9 percent of its budget to these activities (over the country as a whole), Massachusetts provided 26.2 percent of its budget, and the cities and towns allocated less than 1 percent of their own budgets. Looking at expenditures per poor family, the Federal government provided $1,609, the state $1,707, and the localities only $42.[19]

RACE

The Federal presence in racial policy differs from its involvement in transportation and welfare. The national government has not bought state and local cooperation in racial matters as much as it has assumed direct responsibilities where the states and localities have been in-effective, inactive, or negative in their own efforts. The Federal in-volvement came through court decisions, the Civil Rights Acts of 1957–1968, and a series of executive orders. Federal activities seek racial integration in public schools, hospitals, and other government institutions; voting rights; access to such public accommodations as restaurants, theaters, and hotels; and equal opportunities in jobs and housing. The development of national policies toward race illustrates the multiple routes to policy change that are available in the Federal system. Blacks and their white allies faced certain frustration in those states where problems were most visible. The development of national policy did not come easily or through any simple response to altruistic values. The process of national policy making included the movement of blacks in large numbers to the Northern cities, the importance of these Northern black votes to presidential candidates, and presidential appointees to the United States Supreme Court who initiated the modern era in racial policy. Other elements included World War II, which heightened the nation's concern for the horrors of negative racial policies and whose GI Bill provided educational opportunities for a new and larger generation of articulate black leaders.

Racial policies appear in several Federal bills that are not heralded as civil rights acts, i.e., grants-in-aid that direct Federal administrators to enforce racial integration while they distribute funds for schools, hospitals, and other public facilities. Recalcitrant Southern officials face not only the laboriously slow process of Federal court orders, but also the more swift and certain withdrawal of Federal funds. Guidelines that define acceptable rates of integration are anathema for the likes of George Wallace and Lester Maddox. However, the guidelines are not entirely unwelcomed by many professional educators in the South who want a less visible stimulus for integration than the public display of a lawsuit and judicial determination.

Racial policies may appear to be *primarily* Federal, but they are not *entirely* Federal. State efforts—even in the South—complement or exceed the programs of the national government in certain sectors. Also, well-meaning state authorities along with their national counterparts stub their toes on what prove to be difficult to intractable components of racial problems. State efforts include equal opportunity statutes for jobs and housing. By the end of 1967 there were 21 states and localities with fair housing laws of their own.[20] In most cases, however, they ran up against opposition from the private sector and the reluctance of public bodies to employ excessive speed, force, or arbitrary standards. One area of special difficulty is employment. There is discrimination by employers and labor unions, Democrats and Republicans. The situation does not invite Democratic liberalism to oust Republican conservatism. There are disappointments in the numbers and qualifications of black applicants for skilled jobs and the apparent need to discriminate against white applicants in order to hire blacks. The notion of racial quotas is obnoxious to both labor and management, and it runs afoul of the 1964 Civil Rights Act. Efforts to deal in ranges or targets rather than racial quotas generate conflicts in and around agencies that must enforce employment opportunities. The struggles occur in national as well as state governments, and they reflect the numerous administrative details on the route to providing a real piece of the action to a group that has long been on the outside.[21]

There has been an improvement in the political status of blacks that facilitates progress in other areas. Between 1969 and 1975 the number of black elected officials increased by 196 percent. There are now some 3,500 such officials at all levels of government throughout the country, with 55 percent of them in the South. This figure slightly exceeds the South's 53 percent of the country's black population. In that region, the percentage of blacks registered to vote went from 29 in 1960 to 59 in 1971.[22]

No one in his right mind would assert that Southern states would have reached these points on their own volition. Along with Federal provisions, however, individual states and political leaders established creditable records of their own. Most indicative was the support that Georgia's former Governor Jimmy Carter received from black leaders in his campaign for the presidency in 1976. Somewhat more obscure are the records of Lester Maddox and George Wallace. Despite their avowed positions as segregationists, each in his own way earned some praise from black leaders. Both are Populists, and both offered social and economic programs of importance to poor whites and blacks. Both, too, presided over their state governments in a period of increasing black political activity and sophistication, and both saw numerous administrative positions going to black applicants.

One apsect of racial policy where several states perform creditably is their own employment practices. A question that is properly asked about government is: *To what extent does it employ individuals who are discriminated against in the private sector?* The answer has several implications. First, it indicates the commitment of public officials to provide some opportunities to individuals who are socially disadvantaged. This commitment can provide opportunities for employment and even influence over policy for people who are shut out of nongovernmental sectors. Second, public employment can provide the feeling that ethnic minorities will develop their opportunities within the established order rather than by drastic change. The employment policies of government organizations may lessen—or aggravate—whatever tendencies toward nihilism and violence may develop among disadvantaged groups. Third, the employment of individuals from all groups suggests the efforts of government recruiters to search every potential labor market. Where government employment is skewed against disadvantaged groups, large pools of personnel may remain untapped. These pools may require cultivation with special educational and employment opportunities. If they remain unexploited, however, administrative agencies deprive themselves of important resources.

A study by the United States Civil Rights Commission found that state governments did better than the private sector in providing employment opportunities to minorities. In some respects the states and localities combined did better than the Federal government. The Commission surveyed public (Federal, state, and local) and private employment in seven metropolitan areas from around the country during 1967: Atlanta, Baton Rouge, Detroit, Houston, Memphis, Philadelphia, and San Francisco–Oakland.[23] The record of each government depended on the measures used: whether its minority employees were counted in total or in certain highly paid categories and whether its minority employees were compared to minority percentages in the local population or to minority percentages in private employment. For all of the metropolitan areas except Baton Rouge the percentage of blacks in state and local employment combined exceeded the percentages of blacks employed in private industry. In three of the areas (Philadelphia, Atlanta, and Memphis), the percentage of blacks in state and local government employment was higher than the percentage in Federal employment. Generally speaking, local governments did better than the states in providing opportunities to blacks. None of the state governments had as high a percentage of blacks as the central city government in each metropolitan area. In two of the areas, however, the state government had a higher percentage of black employees than the county government.

As in the case of the Federal government, the overwhelming majority of black employees of state and local governments are in the low-paid categories of laborers and other service workers.[24] For some communities, the finding that governments employ a higher percentage of blacks than private industry only means that government rather than the private sector collects the garbage! However, there is a beginning of black employment in the categories of managers, officials, professionals, and technicians. State and local governments in all of the metropolitan areas employed a greater incidence of blacks in these categories than the private sector. In all the metropolitan areas surveyed, about 15 percent of the state employees in these categories were black. State percentages for individual areas ran as high as 30.2 (Detroit), 29.6 (Philadelphia), and 24.4 (Memphis). In these same cities, private sector black employment in these categories was only 4.3, 5.5, and 3.0.[25]

The states are not alone. Some problems in their programs as well as some accomplishments result from ties with the national government. Hundreds of arrangements bind state officials to commitments they—or their predecessors—made with Federal authorities. As we see in the next chapter, other arrangements commit state resources to the support of local operations. The state governments suffer from some of the classic dilemmas of a person caught in the middle: they are bound to (and held responsible for) activities over which they have only partial control.

The Federal nature of American politics allows the national government to buy the states' cooperation with new policy ventures.

However, the Federal mechanisms are not so strong that they insure state responses to Washington's policies. Important variations in state welfare policies, for example, flout 40 years of Federal involvement.

There are positive signs of state vitality despite the constraints of federalism. State governments provide the bulk of the money—and virtually all of the administration—for highway development. There are promising state activities in welfare and racial policies. It would be a mistake, however, to scrap the incentives for program improvement that Federal grants offer to the states. Ours is a system that rests on the expectations that institutions will pursue their own interests and requires other institutions to prod and check their actions. Nothing in this book indicates that the states can be left to go their own way. Likewise, however, nothing indicates that the national government can meet our desires without important reliance on state activities.

NOTES

1 James T. Patterson, *The New Deal and the States: Federalism in Transition* (Princeton, N.J.: Princeton University Press, 1969), chap. 1.

2 Terry Sanford, *Storm over the States* (New York: McGraw-Hill, 1967), pp. 62–63.

3 James L. Sundquist, *Making Federalism Work* (Washington: Brookings, 1969), p. 244.

4 Andrew T. Cowart, "Anti-Poverty Expenditures in the American States: A Comparative Analysis," *Midwest Journal of Political Science* 13 (May 1969), 219–236.

5 David Greenstone and Paul E. Peterson, "Reformers, Machines, and the War on Poverty," in James Q. Wilson, ed., *City Politics and Public Policy* (New York: Wiley, 1968), pp. 267–292.

6 Edward W. Weidner, "Decision-Making in a Federal System," in Aaron Wildavsky, ed., *American Federalism in Perspective* (Boston: Little, Brown, 1967).

7 Patterson, p. 54.

8 Patterson, p. 62.

9 These differences in policy remain even after controlling for economic differences between conservative and progressive states. See Ira Sharkansky, *Regionalism in American Politics* (Indianapolis: Bobbs-Merrill, 1970), chaps. 3 and 6.

10 Ira Sharkansky, *The Routines of Politics* (New York: Van Nostrand Reinhold, 1970).

11 Gilbert Y. Steiner, *Social Insecurity: The Politics of Welfare* (Chicago: Rand McNally, 1966), chap. 6.

12 Steiner, p. 141.

13 For the first crop of serious studies on the uses of revenue-sharing, which detail among other things how difficult it is to determine how the moneys are ultimately employed, see Paul R. Dommel, *The Politics of Revenue Sharing* (Bloomington: Indiana University Press, 1974); Richard P. Nathan, et al., *Monitoring Revenue Sharing* (Washington: Brookings, 1975); Otto G. Stolz, *Revenue-Sharing: Legal and Policy Analysis* (New York: Praeger, 1974); and David A. Caputo and Richard L. Cole, *Urban Politics and Decentralization* (Lexington, Mass.: Heath, 1974).

14 See Phillip C. Burch, *Highway Revenue and Expenditure Policy in the United States* (New Brunswick, N.J.: Rutgers, 1962).

15 Advisory Commission on Intergovernmental Relations, *State Aid to Local Government* (Washington: GPO, 1969), p. 93. This study compares state aids to municipalities (urban) with state aids to counties and townships for rural roads.

16 See Martha Derthick, *The Influence of Federal Grants: Public Assistance in Massachusetts* (Cambridge, Mass.: Harvard, 1970), p. 47; and "Improving the Public Welfare System" (Committee for Economic Development, New York, 1970), p. 50.

17 See James A. Maxwell, *Tax Credits and Intergovernmental Fiscal Relations* (Washington: Brookings, 1962), p. 49.

18 Cowart.

19 Ann F. Friedlaender, "Fiscal Prospects," in Samuel H. Beer and Richard E. Barringer, eds., *The State and the Poor* (Cambridge, Mass.: Winthrop, 1970), especially p. 286.

20 Lynn W. Elery and Thomas W. Casstevens, *The Politics of Fair Housing Legislation* (San Francisco: Chandler, 1968), p. xi. Cited in Harrell Rodgers and Charles Bullock, *Law and Social Change: Civil Rights Laws and Their Consequences* (New York: McGraw-Hill, 1972), chap. 6.

21 See Michael J. Pirre, "Jobs and Training," in Beer and Barringer, eds., pp. 53–83.

22 *Statistical Abstract of the United States, 1975* (Washington: U.S. Government Printing Office, 1975).

23 *For All the People by All the People: A Report on Equal Opportunity in State and Local Government Employment* (Washington: U.S. Commission on Civil Rights, 1969).

24 See Samuel Krislov, *The Negro in Federal Employment: The Quest for Equal Opportunity* (Minneapolis: University of Minnesota Press, 1967).

25 *For All the People by All the People*, pp. 19–23. The Commission on Civil Rights excluded school teachers from their survey. If the teachers had been included, they would have boosted the percentage of blacks employed by state and local governments in professional and managerial categories.

Chapter 6

State Governments and Urban Problems

The cities are the new frontiers and the garbage cans of American society. They present some of the most startling social and economic problems and the most glaring signs of affluence. The wealth and decay of our culture is in the cities. Many more people live in metropolitan areas than in small towns or rural areas. It is now trite to say that America is urban. The votes as well as the wealth and the problems are in the cities, and for these reasons much of our politics is about urban affairs. Almost all of the innovative domestic programs concern the cities. That they have not been able to solve urban problems does not mean that the programs are ill-conceived or mismanaged. It may only mean that many urban problems are too severe or too complex for our intelligence or economic resources.

Any claim that states deal with the major domestic issues of our time must consider the cities. It is not that the states are widely viewed as major contributors to urban programs. Quite the contrary. The states are more often alleged to be the weak element among the three levels of government with respect to urban affairs. One anthology on the subject of state governments and the urban crisis reflects views that are widespread among political scientists, economists, and journalists. In different chapters of this widely regarded book it is written that the states are the "fallen arch" in the governmental systems,[1] that provisions of state constitutions "have inhibited the solution of urban problems in most states,"[2] and that state concerns for the local government needs of metropolitan areas have "been predominantly negative, grudging, road-blocking, or simply indifferent."[3] A highly regarded expert on urban affairs recently told a meeting of the National League of Cities:

> It is rather naive to say that the Federal government usurped states' rights. What has happened is that the state legislatures have committed suicide by not joining the 20th century. . . . For the first 69 years of this century [state governments] have demonstrated their complete and utter disregard for urban problems. . . . By any standards, [the states] are more inept, more subject to special interest pressures, more incompetent to do a job and more corrupt than any other branch of government in the United States.[4]

Critics charge that state taxes drain economic resources from urban areas, that state constitutions do not provide the cities with sufficient legal tools for local authorities to cope with their own problems, and that state agencies avoid the kinds of services that would help urban residents.

It is not difficult to find problems in relationships between state and local governments or in state programs for urban residents. There is much truth in the image of the states as the weak—if not evil—element in the field of urban affairs. During the period of great expansion in Federal aids that began in 1964, the spokespersons of state and local governments competed with one another for their share of the largess.[5] For many years, state governments have viewed the cities as sources of wealth that can be tapped to support programs in small towns and rural areas. However, it is only part of the story to say that the states have failed the cities. The complex nature of urban problems does not allow any simple assessment about the responsibilities of the states or any other level of government. Also, the constitutional and statutory provisions that define state and local relationships do not allow any simple redeployment of state energies. In order to speak fairly about the urban accomplishments, problems, and opportunities of the states, it is necessary to untangle some complexities in the nature of the urban problems and in the elements that keep state governments from mounting any quick and final solution for those problems.

There is some dispute as to whether any major problems are distinctively *urban*. Of course there are unpleasant conditions in the cities, but these are not clearly different from problems that occur elsewhere. Racial discrimination, transportation, education, poverty, health, crime, pollution, unfair taxation, and other labels denote problems that appear in the countryside as well as the city. It is possible—but not certain—that urban variants of these problems are different. The congestion and the magnitude that are endemic to urban settlements may add significant degrees of complexity and seriousness to the general problems of society.

Perhaps the only feature of the urban crisis that is undeniable is the level of controversy it arouses among citizens, government officials, and social scientists. It is a multifaceted crisis that is described in these controversies. At the very least, it includes sharp differences between aspirations and achievements in personal incomes, employment opportunities, racial integration, education, housing, health, crime prevention, and pollution control. At its worst, the crisis is a pitiable failure in all of these fields. If not remedied, the failures may grow into social cancers and destroy our culture. To some people, the various components of the urban crisis fit together into a package of interrelated parts. Some features are said to be more basic than the rest and to present the elementary problems that manifest themselves in numerous ways. From another view, however, the picture is less one of a clear root and several branches than of several problems that may—or may not—relate to one another in various communities.

A VIEW OF URBAN CRISIS

A common view of an urban crisis stresses economic roots.[6] There are lots of people living in the central cities who are poor and who face little immediate hope of leaving their poverty. The most visible feature that is associated with poverty is race. While there are lots of poor white people in the cities, it is the poor blacks who present the most serious concentrations of poverty and who show numerous other discomforts that seem to draw upon—and to feed—their poverty. Blacks show the highest rates of unemployment and underemployment; they are segregated into primary and secondary schools that are said to be "holding pens" more than they are educational institutions preparing graduates for a productive life; their crime and disease rates are the highest in the city; and they have meager opportunities for clean air, clean water, and public recreation. More than any other large group, it is the blacks who suffer from all these elements of an urban crisis:

Educational programs and schoolteachers that are unresponsive to the social and linguistic problems of the urban poor and unable to provide the training necessary to maximize their economic potential

Unemployment concentrations among eighteen to twenty-five-year-old males with little education, making them highly visible and susceptible recruits for civil unrest

Periodic social conflagrations far beyond the control capacities of local police

Dispersal of industrial and commercial jobs to the suburbs, beyond easy commuting range of the central city labor pool

Failure of mass transit to meet the needs of low-income communities for cheap home-to-job transportation

Poor diets resulting in low rates of stamina for school and job performance

High rates of infant mortality and mental retardation, traceable in part to inadequate prenatal care and infant diets

High rates of veneral disease and illegitimacy, with attendant problems of fatherless homes and delinquency passing across generation lines

Substandard housing, plus social and economic barriers against the dispersal of low-income populations to better neighborhoods

High crime rates in poverty neighborhoods, which reflect social dislocations and add to the burdens carried by neighborhood residents

The Federal government receives some of the blame for urban problems. Housing programs for the urban poor and the middle- and upper-income suburbanites produce inequities and a housing sprawl that aggravates existing problems. For the home-owning member of the middle- and upper-income brackets the Federal government provides mortgage subsidies under the programs of the Veterans Administration and the Federal Housing Administration, plus further subsidies from the Internal Revenue Service in the form of income-deductibility of mortgage interest and property tax payments. These programs stimulate suburban growth and the emigration of high taxpayers from the central city, leaving a residue of blight. For the urban poor there are meager funds for low-rent public housing. In 1968 the President's Commission on Civil Disorders asked for 6 million low- and moderate-income housing units over a 5-year period. During 1966–1968, the average annual number of public-assisted housing starts was only 71,000 units.[7] From 1969 to 1974, the number of low-rent public housing units (including those under management, under construction, or in the planning stage) increased by only 279,000. One study found that Federal programs to subsidize housing for the poorest one-fifth of the population cost $820 million in 1962, while the same year's programs to subsidize housing for the wealthiest one-fifth of the population cost $1.7 billion.[8]

A BRIGHTER VIEW OF THE URBAN SCENE

Along with the frequent citations of urban problems and despair, there is another view which contends that *things are not as bad as they seem*, and *they are better than ever before*.

> The plain fact is that the overwhelming majority of city dwellers live more comfortably and conveniently than ever before. They have more and better housing, more and better schools, more and better transportation, and so on. By any conceivable measure of material welfare the present generation of urban Americans is, on the whole, better off than any other large group of people has ever been anywhere. What is more, there is every reason to expect that the general level of comfort and convenience will continue to rise at an even more rapid rate through the foreseeable future.[9]

This quotation summarizes a major argument in Edward C. Banfield's *The Unheavenly City*. He does not quarrel with the presence of an urban crisis, but defines the crisis in terms of frustrated expectations rather than objective indicators of deprivation. Banfield finds that the problems of poverty, ignorance, disease, poor housing, and crime affect "only a rather small minority of the whole urban population."[10] Moreover, some of the problems are necessary accompaniments of the attractions of urban society. Congestion will not go away as long as many people find great benefits in living so close to many other people and the jobs and commercial and cultural opportunities that occur in urban areas. Traffic snarls will remain as long as people resist staggered hours of employment in favor of a 9 to 5 routine.

Banfield does not deny the presence of segregation, inadequate housing, and poverty in urban areas, but he claims that conditions are better than in rural areas. The vast majority of inadequate housing exists *outside* large cities. Education levels are, to be sure, lower in central cities than in the suburbs. But they are lower in rural areas than in central cities. The urban police are intemperate in their dealings with blacks and other ethnic minorities, but not to the extent of the sheriff in the rural South.

Banfield looks at some of the alleged problems in urban areas and finds them grossly exaggerated. In the place of claims about unprecedented population growth in low-income neighborhoods, he cites greater immigration of the poor in earlier decades of urban history. To those who argue that vast numbers of poor blacks will overcome the city's capacity for economic and social accommodation, Banfield argues that earlier decades of southern European peasant migration placed larger strains—proportionate to the existing population and economic base—on urban political systems.

There are urban problems that concern Banfield. One is the unprecedented concentration of an urban black population whose psychological alienation from the dominant society may be far greater than suggested by the indices of material deprivation. The young males especially provide a pool of unemployed labor with bleak economic prospects. While their condition may be no worse economically—and actually better—than that of their rural forebears, their concentrations in urban ghettoes provide the critical human mass that may explode and threaten our basic social fabric. Second is the gap between *anticipated* social and economic gains and the benefits *actually obtained*. Insofar as aspirations grow faster than accomplishments, this gap may continue to enlarge. No matter how much social progress is measured, there remains the tinder for a social revolution. Third, governments pursue activities that are unable to solve basic social and personal problems but whose presence helps to increase aspirations and thus pave the way for frustrations.

To a large extent . . . our urban problems are like the mechanical rabbit at the racetrack, which is set to keep just ahead of the dogs no matter how fast they may run. Our performance is better and better, but because we set our standards and expectations to keep ahead of performance, the problems are never any nearer to solution. . . .

The effect of too-high standards cannot be to spur us on to reach the prescribed level of performance sooner than we otherwise would, for that level is by definition impossible of attainment. At the same time, these standards may cause us to adopt measures that are wasteful and injurious and, in the long run, to conclude from the inevitable failure of these measures that there is something fundamentally wrong with our society.[11]

Banfield makes a persuasive case that certain things about the cities have never been better. Yet he concedes that achievements have not reached aspirations and may even be falling further behind. Even this brighter view of the city is discouraging. Social progress is not only measured by what is, but by what could be.

THE IRONY OF URBAN WEALTH

A persistent irony in the urban scene—and a feature that complicates any assessment of state responsibility for current urban problems—is the juxtaposition of enormous wealth in the private sector with apparent poverty in the public sector.[12] Urban areas contain fantastic wealth at the same time that municipalities and school districts cry poverty. The wealth of human and material resources in the metropolis should make social problems more amenable to solution. There is lots of money in the cities and lots of people with the skills needed to plan and implement social programs. Also, the people needing help are concentrated in a relatively small space and could be reached in an efficient manner by well-designed programs. To understand *if* state governments have failed in their urban responsibilities and *how they might improve* their urban-oriented programs, it is necessary to assess the wealth that is contained in urban areas and to ask why it is not sufficient to deal with the problems that surround it.

The population growth of urban areas is one sign of their economic prosperity. However, their growth also presents difficulties for urban authorities. Many of the people who are caught in the urban crisis came to the city for the economic opportunities it promised. Urban prosperity attracts the untrained and unsuccessful who want better opportunities for themselves and their families. For some newcomers, the cost to the city of providing them with services is substantially greater than the contribution of their skills to the city's economy. Urban slums represent a combination of several things: the attractions of the city for poor people; the inability of many immigrants to be successful in the urban environment; and the costs to urban communities of their own economic attractions. This is the irony of the urban economy: an abundance of wealth that begets poverty even while it reproduces wealth and a magnitude of resources that is not sufficient for local authorities to satisfy the intense demands that they receive.

Today's unskilled migrants encounter frustrations that mercifully escaped their predecessors. The urban economy used to have lots of room for unskilled workers. Factories were more dependent upon hand labor than they are today; municipal governments employed large numbers of menial laborers; and there were many unskilled construction jobs in the growing cities. Dropouts could easily find gainful employment. There are still many of these opportunities, but their proportion in the urban economy is diminishing steadily. Literacy is increasingly a requirement for even the lowest paid and least stable jobs. The spread of the labor movement and union control of apprenticeship programs means that today's ethnic newcomers suffer from the institutionalized discrimination of co-workers as well as from that of prospective employers.

TOO MANY LOCAL GOVERNMENTS

The fractured nature of local government in urban areas is an important element in limiting the revenue available to local governments. Multiple boundaries divide the urban area into a surplus of jurisdictions. Often they compete with each other to keep taxes low. Some local jurisdictions have a greater tax base than required to support their services, so their tax bills can be low. Other jurisdictions have needs that surpass their resources. While they may raise taxes to the legal or political limits, there remains untapped resources in neighboring jurisdictions.

Many of the contrasts in urban resources and service demands distinguish the central city from the suburbs and one suburb from another. A study of Detroit, for example, found that 25 suburban school districts spent up to $500 *more per child* per year to educate their children than did the City of Detroit. In the core city area of Detroit, nearly a third of the public school buildings were built during the administration of President Ulysses S. Grant.[13] Another study found a New Jersey community with an assessed valuation of $5.5 million per pupil, while a neighboring community had a valuation of $33,000 per pupil.[14]

POLITICS OF METROPOLITAN REFORM: INTEGRATE
THE SURPLUS OF GOVERNMENTS

It is difficult to identify a state responsibility in the problems of governing metropolitan areas. There are sharp disagreements among local people about what should be done and many urbanites who want things to remain in their present condition. Some urban reformers advocate a reduction in the surplus of local governments. They assert that rational public policy requires at least a minimum of coordination. Separate communities in the metropolis cannot realize all the benefits of coherent policy and the consequent economies of scale which larger units can secure. Different jurisdictions too often segregate economic resources from program needs. Reformers have attempted ten varieties of local government integration:

1 Municipal regulation of real estate developments in the rural fringe outside its borders
2 Intergovernmental agreements
3 Voluntary metropolitan councils
4 The urban county
5 Transfer of functions to state governments
6 Metropolitan special districts
7 Annexation and city-city consolidation
8 Separation of the urbanized area into a city distinct for all purposes from the rural elements in its former county
9 Consolidation of the city with the urbanized county surrounding it
10 Federation of several municipalities[15]

Measured by the oceans of ink spilled by the reform advocates, these efforts are only modestly successful. Several patterns appear in the numerous failures and few successes:

1. Public officials and the power structure of the metropolitan area rarely initiate reform proposals. The typical proposal for metropolitan reform starts in the private sector with help from such groups as the League of Women Voters, civic betterment associations, newspapers, or unattached intellectuals. Established local officials reached their positions within the existing structure and accommodate themselves to its opportunities. In Cleveland, for example, support for governmental reform came from business associations, labor unions, and even political parties, while opposition came from elected officials of central city and suburban governments. Without the support of the elected officials at the peaks of central city and suburban governments, reform proposals begin with an important strike against them.

2. Voters are apathetic about metropolitan organization and place higher valuations upon other goals (e.g., community autonomy). If public officials are relatively unconcerned about reorganization, voters seem even less enthusiastic. Studies of several metropolitan areas[16] show that citizens (except for residents of racial ghettos[17]) are satisfied with existing municipal services. Voters seem to be more impressed by arguments concerning a loss of community autonomy in the suburbs and a fear of higher taxes than by the abstract arguments in favor of metropolitan consolidation.

3. Voter information concerning metropolitan reform tends to be minimal, inaccurate, or both. Less than a third of the electorate in one effort to integrate Miami governments had heard of the reform proposal and had even minimal understanding of it.[18]

4. Political party leaders tend to be either apathetic or antagonistic to change. Most central cities of large metropolitan areas outside the South are Democratic while their suburbs are Republican. The merging of central cities and fringe areas would almost certainly decrease predictability for local party leaders. In most areas it would benefit the Republican party. As Banfield writes, "even if the proportion of Republicans declines sharply in the suburbs, metropolitan government north of the Mason-Dixon line would almost everywhere be Republican government. In effect, advocates of consolidation schemes are asking the Democrats to give up their control of the central cities, or at least to place it in jeopardy."[19] Related to the opposition of Democratic party leaders and municipal officials is the finding that:

5. Metropolitan reform proposals are often opposed by labor unions.

6. Black leaders and voters are usually opposed to reorganization. In a succession of 10 reorganization proposals over a 25-year period in Cleveland, the incidence of black opposition increased with each election.[20] This increasing black opposition to metropolitan reform occurred with an increase in the proportion of blacks in the city electorate, culminating in the 1967 election of Carl Stokes as mayor. In Cleveland and other large cities, metropolitan reform would dilute the strength of blacks in the newly enlarged electorate.

The facts warrant this emphasis on the elements that discourage metropolitan reform. Out of 47 referendums on metropolitan reorganization, undertaken in 36 of the nation's 212 Standard Metropolitan Statistical Areas during 1946–1968, only 18 produced favorable votes. Even this figure overstates the success of reform campaigns. It reports only those campaigns where reform forces were strong enough to put the issue on the ballot. In the largest metropolitan areas, few major reforms have even been undertaken. Most successes occurred in small- to medium-sized cities in border states. Governmental change is easiest where the problems are moderate and the opposition to change is correspondingly weak. The batting average of reform looks better on paper than it does in reality.

POLITICS OF METROPOLITAN REFORM: WE NEED MORE LOCAL GOVERNMENTS

After reading the preceding section, we might ask: Why doesn't the state government add its weight to the movement for metropolitan integration? That question is premature, however, and assumes that there are no arguments against government integration.

Some observers find merit in the existing pattern of numerous local authorities which offer varying choices of tax and service packages. A metropolitan resident can now select what seems most suitable among the localities on the basis of services and tax levies, as well as on criteria of location, scenery, and the social characteristics of the population. There are also some research findings that argue against the integration of governments throughout a metropolis: small- and medium-sized police, school, and sanitation departments in the suburbs can offer a higher quality of service. They can also adapt more rapidly to shifting demands than the sprawling bureaucracies of the central cities and, presumably, more rapidly than the even larger bureaucracies that would result from metropolitan reforms.[21]

Another argument against metropolitan integration appears in the persistent opposition to urban consolidation that is shown by black voters. Ghetto leaders argue—probably rightly—that expansions of municipal borders will dilute the voting strength they have acquired in central cities. They represent a theme in local politics that runs directly counter to metropolitan consolidation: demands for *more local governments in metropolitan areas!* Blacks are powerful blocs in Cleveland, Newark, Gary, New York City, Washington, Chicago, Los Angeles, and other cities. It is the concentration of blacks into ghetto neighborhoods of central cities that provides them with clout in local elections. Their concentration also supports their claims for submunicipal autonomy.

This movement goes by several names: "decentralization," "neighborhood control," "community control," "control-sharing." Not all devices for decentralization are similar. There are important differences between arrangements that *actually decentralize* the power to make program decisions and arrangements that merely *provide representation on a centralized policy-making body to program clients.*[22] Their differences extend not only to the amount of power the municipal government would surrender (it would surrender more under "decentralization") but also to the extent that each arrangement seems likely to produce services that are designed for the needs of different locales within the city and produce satisfaction in the local communities. Presumably there would be more individualized programming and more local satisfaction with decentralization than with client representation.

The move toward additional local governments is not entirely a black phenomenon. It finds support from residents of upper-income white areas who want special opportunities to create educational and recreational facilities suitable to their desires. Any effort to explain the move toward additional governments *within* central cities must take account of the earlier blossoming of suburban governments. Many spokespersons for inner-city decentralization justify their demands by reference to the suburbs. Ghetto leaders want for themselves the benefits of local autonomy.

Although decentralization has an innovative and even revolutionary image in urban areas, it is not original in American history. It is consistent with our willingness to build more governments when we face new demands for public service. It resembles, in these terms, the multiplication of suburban municipalities that have grown since the 1920s and in greater numbers since World War II. Decentralization reflects de Tocqueville's observations about the attachments of Americans to their local governments. What applied to the white yeoman of the nineteenth century, and to the white suburbanite of the first half of the twentieth century, applies also to the black ghetto dweller of the late twentieth century. What contemporary movements for decentralization do to state officials, however, is to raise the political costs of any state-initiated move to consolidate local governments in metropolitan areas. It is difficult to mount any reform when intense advocates stand at the polar extremes of fewer governments versus more governments.

The fractured nature of government in metropolitan areas is only one of the problems that complicates the lives of state officials and hinders the easy translation of the city's private affluence into adequate government budgets. Other problems come from the historic dependence of state programs on funds taken out of the cities and from the tangled statutes that define state-local relationships. Even if state governments wanted to rush pell mell into the cities and provide massive help, there are years of accumulated law, tradition, habit, and commitment that would have to change. These are *not* features that encourage the states to help the cities. They are vestiges of a rural era that hinder the cities' capacity to help themselves. One of the traditional state-urban relationships is a historic legacy of the wealth found in urban areas: state constitutions and laws restrict the funds that cities can raise for their own purposes and require that city taxpayers contribute to state coffers so that "poorer" rural areas may receive intergovernmental assistance. Undoubtedly, urban areas should continue as the fiscal crutch of poor hinterlands. Yet anachronistic formulas in certain state aids provide greater benefits to wealthy suburbs than to struggling core cities. With the cities caught between the movement of big corporate taxpayers to the suburbs and the competition from state tax systems that do not return fair shares, city schools and other services seem helpless in the face of the natives' demands. Remember, however, that existing allocations of state aids favor some groups while they annoy others. There would be losers as well as gainers from changes in policy and, as a result, change will not come easily.

STATE PROGRAMS FOR URBAN AREAS

By now it is clear that urban residents have problems. Not the least of these are the enormous problems in defining what is wrong, and who is responsible for it. There is dispute over the existence of problems that are distinctively *urban*; ironic complications of law and economics that hinder the translation of urban wealth into public resources for urban needs; and a miasma of governmental responsibilities plus contrary recommendations for change (more governments versus fewer governments) that becloud any effort to rationalize policy making for urban areas.

It is time to ask what the state governments are doing for the urban areas. Clearly the state governments are not doing enough. No government is. That is evident to all who see that social and economic discomforts remain. It is debatable, however, whether any (or all) governments could solve urban problems through public action. Because of confusions as to the nature and solubility of the problems (which are the economic problems and which are the problems of mass frustration?) we cannot come to an absolute judgment about the goodness or badness of state programs. We can, however, evaluate state actions by seeing what they are doing now in comparison to what they did in the past. Are there changes in the direction of showing more concern for problems in urban areas? And are the changes of sufficient magnitude to suggest that the states are making serious efforts for their urban responsibilities? Two kinds of information are relevant to these questions: (1) The amount of state financial aid to urban governments and (2) the kinds of services provided by state agencies to urban residents and urban governments.

We conceded in Chapter 3 that money alone is not the whole answer to social problems. However, money is one of the things governments provide to those who know some of the answers. State government can help people in the cities with financial aids to local authorities. Because urban areas are fractured by the boundaries of numerous jurisdictions, many local governments have too few taxable resources within their own borders. And because they are confined to a limited number of revenue devices (i.e., property taxes and service charges) they cannot raise sufficient revenues on their own. State aid is an attractive answer. The state government taxes the wealth of an entire metropolitan area without regard to local government boundaries. Moreover, state aid can avoid the intractable problems of metropolitan reform. The suburbs, central city, and special districts may continue to mouth the values of individuality and parochialism, while state aids make up for the revenue problems that come from a lack of integration among metropolitan governments.

There is no guarantee that state aid will be adequate for the needs of urban governments. That depends partly on how much aid is made available, and how it is allocated among local governments. The record on both these points is promising. State payments to local governments show a considerable and growing concern for urban problems. The states aid the cities far more than the national government does. Moreover, state aids are going in increasing amounts to cities that need help the most.

If we accept the assumption that social and economic problems are more complex in the larger cities, then we should applaud the distribution of state aids. State aids to large cities are substantially greater than to medium- and small-sized cities.[23] Table 6-1 shows per capita aids of $266.65 in the largest cities (over one million in population) during 1973–1974 and only $32.82 in the smallest cities (under 50,000 in population). Moreover, state aids bulked larger in the budgets of the bigger cities: 35.3 percent in the largest cities and 17.7 percent in the smallest cities.

State aids show *increasing* attention to large cities. From 1960 to 1973–1974, per capita aids to cities over one million population increased by more than seven times, and they almost doubled as a percentage of the cities' budgets. In contrast, state aids to cities with less than 50,000 population increased less than four times in per capita terms, and they remained virtually unchanged as a percentage of city budgets. To the extent that money is a fair index of state government concern for urban problems, there is considerable evidence for that concern in state aids to the largest municipalities.[24]

The states are not alone in providing financial aid to local governments. From 1961 to 1975, Federal aids spent in metropolitan areas

Table 6-1   State Aids to City Governments, 1960 and 1973-1974

	1960		1973-1974	
City size	Per capita state aid	State aid as percentage of city revenue	Per capita state aid	State aid as percentage of city revenue
1,000,000 plus	$35.95	17.8	$266.65	35.3
500,000-999,999	23.48	16.4	86.18	18.3
300,000-499,999	14.11	13.2	72.84	19.7
200,000-299,999	12.28	11.4	68.26	19.1
100,000-199,999	14.77	14.2	59.68	18.9
50,000-99,999	13.91	15.0	46.93	17.5
25,000-49,999	11.27	14.3	32.82	17.7
less than 25,000	8.62	17.0		

Sources: U.S. Bureau of the Census, *Compendium of City Government Finances in 1960* (and *1973-1974*) (Washington: GPO, 1961 and 1975).

increased by almost 10 times: from $3.9 to $35.9 billion.[25] Much of this Federal money goes to the state governments, and it is state agencies that allocate it to the ultimate recipients. Local governments receive far more in state aid than in money that comes direct from Washington. Local governments received $10.2 billion in direct Federal aid and $44.6 billion in state aid during 1973-1974.

An increasing number of states are changing their constitutions to permit local governments greater freedom in raising their own revenues. Historically, the localities have been confined to the property tax. As noted earlier, this suffers from its regressivity and from sharp political hostility. As of 1974, local governments in 29 states collected a sales tax, and local governments in 10 states collected an income tax. In most cases, the city council or county board defines a tax rate from the options made available by the state legislature; then a state agency collects the funds, audits taxpayers' returns, and sends the money to local governments.

Additional state programs improve the administration of local property taxes. Forty states make periodic comparisons between market values (as determined by actual sales) and local property assessments. These "sales-assessment ratios" are used to equalize state aids to local governments (many aid programs go to communities on the basis of local property values). Thirty states also use the sales-assessment ratios to determine which areas need additional attention for tax assessors. In this way the state puts a damper on tax competition between local governments. If the state program works well, it should keep local assessments reasonably equivalent across the state for properties of similar value.[26]

NEW YORK'S FINANCIAL PROBLEMS: 1975 AND 1976

No consideration of state aids for local governments can be complete without dealing with the financial difficulties of New York City that came to a head in 1975, despite the fact that the outcome of this affair has not been reached and its implications for Federal, state, and local relations are not entirely clear.

By the middle of 1975 it was apparent that New York City faced the results of having exceeded financial prudence over a number of years. There remained nothing but unpleasant alternatives: to make unprecedented reductions in public services and civil service payrolls; to go into bankruptcy, which would have unknown implications for creditors, government employees, and service recipients; or to engineer some unique combination of measures, with their details dependent on actions taken by New York State and the national government. By the end of 1975 the city's finances were so tangled with those of New York State that a City bankruptcy could have meant a State bankruptcy. Even the threat of a New York City bankruptcy sent shock waves through the bond markets. Other cities and states—even those with sound balances—found it impossible to sell bonds at reasonable rates of interest. European governments brought pressure to bear on the White House to help out the City. They suggested that international financial confidence in the United States could falter, with the consequence being a deeper world depression, if the nation's most prominent city was allowed to go under. On the other side, there were arguments against special Federal aid by those who feared dire consequences for the proper balance of the Federal system.

With the national government reluctant to help (one New York *Daily News* headline read: FORD TO CITY: DROP DEAD), the burden of aid and control rested on New York State. The State's measures included:

1 Creation of a special financial device, the Municipal Assistance Corporation, to use the State's credit rating to borrow funds for the City.

2 Creation of an Emergency Financial Control Board to oversee City finances, including the State's demands for trimmed services, layoffs, new taxes, and a balanced budget within 3 years.

3 Arrangements for additional loans from public pension funds and private lenders and establishment of more cuts in city services and payrolls, after it became apparent that the Municipal Assistance Corporation could not borrow the required funds without endangering the State's own finances.

Here we see a state government using its powers to reorder the finances of a municipal government that had overextended its generosity to the point of insolvency. It is not hard to find examples of the City's generosity to its citizens and employees: coin changers in the subway received $229 per week while bank clerks were being paid $164; police officers on the job 3 years earned $17,458; a 1974 survey by the U.S. Bureau of the Census found the average monthly earnings of New York City employees to be $1,156, while those of employees in 74 other major metropolitan areas was only $1,005. Many employees hired before 1974 could retire after 20 years on the job with pensions one-half their last year's earnings. This provision made it possible for a worker to retire in his or her early forties with a $15,000 pension, plus the opportunity to work at another job for 25 or so additional years. While students at public universities around the country were paying an average $552 per year for tuition and fees, those enrolled at the City University of New York were charged fees of only $110.

Administrative control was not a strong point for the city. Various journalists reported that no one knew exactly how many people worked for the city; estimates ranged from 295,500 to 400,000. And while it cost the city some $45 per ton to collect garbage, the same task was done by private contractors for $22 a ton in San Francisco, $19 a ton in Boston, and $18 a ton in Minneapolis.

By 1975 the city could not meet costs like these with available revenues. With State pressures leading a chorus of demands from bondholders, Federal officials, and outraged citizens, the city stopped some $1 billion worth of construction, closed hospitals, eliminated subsidies to museums and theaters, froze wages or postponed expected increases in salaries, reduced its civil service by some 45,000 personnel, levied its first tuition charges at the City University of New York, and closed the entire institution for a time in May 1976 when its coffers ran dry. Swallowing this kind of medicine is hard for any government and shows the capacity of a state government to take as well as to give in its relations with cities.

STATE INFLUENCES ON THE QUALITY OF URBAN LIFE

What of state programs—other than financial aids—that may improve the quality of urban life? Some of these programs are outside the scope of this chapter: Chapters 4 and 5 describe efforts in higher education, highways, welfare, and race. Nowhere in this book can we provide any thorough discussion of state programs in the fields of mental health, public safety, and environmental control that benefit urban residents. An increasing number of states support local programs in mental health or locate state clinics and hospitals in metropolitan areas. More and more states are investing heavily in urban colleges and universities, state parkland in metropolitan areas, and express highways that link various parts of metropolitan areas. Almost all the states operate training classes for local property assessors, police officers, health inspectors, and public works engineers. The extension divisions of state universities conduct many of these programs.

If the states have been negligent in the field of environmental control, it is due partly to the interstate nature of many air- and water-sheds and the desirability of Federal action. Now the states are on the bandwagon. Even Maine, a small and low-income state historically dependent on the pollution-prone industries of logging and papermaking, has enacted an environmental protection law that is cited as a model by other states. We should not forget California's pioneering efforts in smog control that set the stage for massive Federal programs.

Several states offer imaginative housing programs. Massachusetts passed a "snob zoning law," designed to thwart the efforts of local communities to exclude low- and moderate-income housing. The law establishes a Housing Appeals Committee with power to override decisions of local zoning boards. The bill's supporters see it as a tool to permit low-income and black residents outside congested central cities. More mundane in appearance but of potentially great significance are statewide building codes adopted in Massachusetts and Virginia. Such codes supersede the great variety of local codes which impede the use of standardized components, retard innovation in building techniques, and often inflate building costs for homeowners and renters.

A harsh judgment of the states would say that programs to help local authorities are barely underway despite the long-standing nature of urban problems. In other words, "It is about time" and "The states are doing little even now." A more balanced assessment would emphasize the recent spurt in state programs and the breadth of services that several states provide; it would also recognize the controversial elements that surround urban politics and complicate any governments' effort to solve the problems.

Most states have administrative units to aid local governments. Almost all are creatures of the late 1960s. Only two states had such units before 1960 (Alaska and New York). Before 1965, 2 more units appeared and then 26 more agencies during 1965-1969. Some of these agencies channel state financial aid to local governments. Most of them aid local governments with technical assistance. "Technical assistance" is a catch-all label that covers training for local personnel, advice in a range of matters from property tax assessment to pollution control, and assistance in applying for Federal aid. Some state agencies provide staff services for local governments that the recipients might otherwise have to provide themselves, e.g., land-use planning and public works engineering. The most advanced of the new agencies offer sizable financial supplements to urban programs of the Federal government: public housing, mass transit, urban renewal, and manpower training.

In some ways state governments have helped their cities simply by allowing them more discretion in governing themselves. More states are allowing their cities to collect income and sales taxes. An increasing number of urban counties have acquired greater controls over their affairs. Kentucky loosened its reins on the City of Louisville in 1972-1973 and New Jersey—the country's most completely urban state—offered four optional forms of government to its counties. These and similar enactments elsewhere remind us that state governments offer a variety of benefits for their urban areas: freedom from outmoded controls as in these cases; an assertion of control over a city that has gotten itself into trouble as in the case of New York; more financial aid as in the case of just about all states; and the direct provision of state services in urban areas.

It may be true that this chapter devotes more space to the nature of urban problems than to the urban accomplishments of state governments. Historically, the forte of state governments was farm-to-market roads, agricultural research, plus colleges and hospitals in bucolic settings. The urban benefits from state programs lie as much in the category of potential as in accomplishment.

In describing the variety of state actions in behalf of localities, this chapter offers a picture of what is possible. And by showing the increase in financial aids—especially those going to the largest cities—it provides a summary measure of the direction that state governments have taken in recent years.

NOTES

1 Alan K. Campbell and Donna E. Shalala, "Problems Unsolved, Solutions Untried: The Urban Crisis," in Alan K. Campbell, ed., *The States and the Urban Crisis* (Englewood Cliffs, N.J.: Prentice-Hall, 1970), p. 6.

2 Frank P. Grad, "The State's Capacity to Respond to Urban Problems: The State Constitution," in Alan K. Campbell, *The States and the Urban Crisis*, p. 27.

3 Daniel R. Grant, "Urban Needs and State Response: Local Government Reorganization," in Alan K. Campbell, *The States and the Urban Crisis*, pp. 74–75.

4 Philip M. Hauser, "Whither the Urban Society?" an address to the National League of Cities, San Diego, California, December 2, 1969. Mimeo.

5 See Donald H. Haider, *When Governments Come to Washington: Governors, Mayors, and Intergovernmental Lobbying* (New York: Free Press, 1974).

6 This section relies on Robert L. Lineberry and Ira Sharkansky, *Urban Politics and Public Policy* (New York: Harper, 1977).

7 Campbell and Shalala, pp. 14–15.

8 Alvin Schorr, "National Community and Housing Policy," *The Social Service Review*, 39 (December 1965), quoted in Campbell and Shalala, pp. 13–14.

9 Edward C. Banfield, *The Unheavenly City* (Boston: Little, Brown, 1970), pp. 3–4. The revised edition of Banfield's book, *The Unheavenly City Revisited*, published in 1974, does not depart in any significant way from the ideas discussed in the first edition.

10 Banfield, p. 11.

11 Banfield, pp. 21–22.

12 This section relies on Lineberry and Sharkansky.

13 *Report* of the National Commission on Civil Disorders (Washington: GPO, 1968), p. 241.

14 Robert C. Wood, *1400 Governments* (Garden City, N.Y.: Anchor Books, 1961), p. 55.

15 Advisory Commission Intergovernmental Relations, *Alternative Approaches to Governmental Reorganization in Metropolitan Areas* (Washington: GPO, 1962). This section relies on Robert L. Lineberry, "Reforming Metropolitan Government: Requiem or Reality?" *Georgetown Law Journal*, 58 (May 1970).

16 See John Bollens et al., *Exploring the Metropolitan Community* (Berkeley: University of California Press, 1963), pp. 188–190.

17 *Report* of the National Commission on Civil Disorders, pp. 79–83.

18 Edward Sofen, *The Miami Metropolitan Experiment* (Bloomington: University of Indiana Press, 1963), p. 74.

19 Edward C. Banfield, "The Politics of Metropolitan Area Organization," *Midwest Journal of Political Science*, 1 (May 1957), pp. 77–91.

20 Richard A. Watson and John H. Romani, "Metropolitan Government for Metropolitan Cleveland," *Midwest Journal of Political Science*, 5 (November 1961), pp. 365–390.

21 See Vincent Ostrom, "The Study of Federalism at Work," *Publius: The Journal of Federalism* (Fall 1974), pp. 1–18; Vincent Ostrom, "Can Federalism Make a Difference?" *Publius: The Journal of Federalism* (Fall 1973), pp. 197–238; and Elinor Ostrom et al., "Defining and Measuring Structural Variations in Intergovernmental Arrangements," *Publius: The Journal of Federalism* (Fall 1974), pp. 87–108.

22 Peter K. Eisinger, "Control Sharing of Administrative Functions in the City," a paper delivered at the 1970 Annual Meeting of the American Political Science Association, Los Angeles.

23 Not all activities conducted by local governments in urban areas are operated by cities (or municipalities). Counties, school districts, and other special districts each operate important programs. There are different findings for state aids to *local* governments than for aids to *city* governments. The information available directs attention to state aids for *city* governments. State aids to cities actually show the weaker arguments for the value of state aids; state aids account for 31.1 percent of all local governments' revenues (as of 1973–1974), but only 19.8 percent of city

governments' revenues. Approximately 60 percent of state aids
go to school districts, many of which are outside urban areas. To
the credit of the state governments, however, an increasing proportion of school aids are distributed in a way to compensate
for inadequate financial resources in the local communities. Over
the country as a whole, 69.2 percent of state aids for education
were distributed in a way to compensate for economic conditions
in the recipient school districts in 1966–1967. This compared
with only 47.7 percent so distributed to compensate for economic conditions in 1953–1954. See: Advisory Commission on
Intergovernmental Relations, *State Aid to Local Government*
(Washington: GPO, 1969), p. 57.

24   To some extent, the larger state aids to the largest cities reflect
the inclusion of school funds in the budgets of those cities. However, this distortion does not account for all the relative growth
in the state aids of these cities over the 1960–1973–1974 period.
In this period, the school and nonschool budgets of the largest
cities have benefited from state aids more than the budgets of
the smallest cities. A careful comparison of the figures in the
first and second editions of this book will show that state aid
has increased somewhat more for certain categories of medium-
sized and smaller cities than for certain categories of larger cities
in the period 1968–1969 to 1973–1974. In this period, the cities
receiving the largest new increments were those in the 300,000
to 500,000 population range. This may reflect the peaking of
the political weight of the largest cities in the middle and late
1960s, a period coinciding with their success nationally during
the administration of President Lyndon Johnson.

25   *Budget of the United States: Special Analyses, Fiscal Year 1975*
(Washington: GPO, 1974), p. 229.

26   Advisory Commission on Intergovernmental Relations, *State and
Local Finances: Significant Features 1967 to 1970* (Washington:
GPO, 1969), pp. 126–127.

Chapter 7

Where Do the States Go from Here?

Too many people malign the states unjustly. State governments are not weak elements in the Federal system. They provide an increasing portion of the money for domestic services. During recent years when the national government has diverted its attention elsewhere and the local governments have faced persistent opposition to their property taxes, the states have increased their own share of the financial burden. Between 1959 and 1970 there were 410 increases in the major states' taxes. From 1970 to 1974, state taxes increased by another 55 percent, while Federal and local tax receipts increased by only 39 percent.

The states gained dominance over the private sector in the field of higher education. Not only do they serve increased enrollments, but they provide increasingly specialized and expensive services, and they deal—no less successfully than private institutions—with the controversial demands and tactics of an aggressive younger generation. Even in fields where the national government seems to dominate (transportation, welfare, and race), many state governments do their own share. States

raise most of the funds that are spent on highways, and it is state administrators who face the social and political problems that come with
highway construction. Individual states make impressive efforts in public
welfare, sometimes in stark contrast to their meager levels of economic
resources. Race is the historic weakness of state governments. Yet race
is also a weakness of the national and local governments. It is not a
problem that is easily faced or resolved. State governments in all parts
of the country deserve some credit for their racial policies. In each of
the seven metropolitan areas surveyed by the United States Commission
on Civil Rights, state agencies employed a higher proportion of blacks
in professional and managerial positions than private enterprise. In
three of these areas, state and local governments combined did better
than the local offices of the Federal government.

Urban policies remain as the target of the states' most severe critics.
Even in this field, however, there are some impressive accomplishments
and promising signs for the future. There is a real dispute as to how
much of the urban crisis is the responsibility of the state governments.
Just looking at the portion of the crisis that falls within the category of
"insufficient funds," the states share the responsibility with local and
national officials. It is partly because of fragmented governments in
metropolitan areas that cities cannot raise adequate revenues from the
urban economy. The failure of local government consolidation is not so
much the responsibility of state governments as it is the preference of
local citizens and officials. Reorganization proposals seldom get on the
ballot in metropolitan areas and seldom win when they do reach the
ballot. Now an increased respect for multiple options and demands for
decentralization within the core cities may spell the end of metropolitan consolidation as the favorite gimmick of governmental reformers. Over the past few years, state officials have assumed an
increasing share of the financial responsibilities for urban as well as
other programs. The states no longer view the cities as pots of gold to
support programs in rural areas. Present state aids favor the large cities
and are moving increasingly in that direction. While state aids to cities
have increased, the local governments' own share of government spending for domestic programs has gone down. The Federal government's
share has increased, but less than the states' share. In various sectors of
public service, the states are looking increasingly to the needs of urban
residents in higher education, mental health, environmental control,

recreation, highways, mass transit, and housing. Most of the states have departments of local affairs with explicit missions to help their urban areas.

It is appropriate to step back from the record of recent developments and ask which of them will continue. Some modest predictions are appropriate. The forecasts reflect features of state policy that are already apparent. What may come onto the stage after this is beyond the grasp of intelligence.

Four major trends are visible:

1 State tax systems will continue to provide a large—and probably increasing—portion of the funds to support domestic programs.

2 The national government will retain important commitments overseas that keep the full weight of its fiscal capacity from domestic programs.

3 Urban areas will continue as the locales where social and economic problems take their most tangible and visible forms, and they will increasingly receive the attention of state governments.

4 State investments in higher education may cease their rapid upswing as student enrollments no longer show the massive increases of the 1960s.

Each of the first three trends predicts extensions of the recent past, i.e., more of the same. In the fourth category there is some contrary evidence. Not that expenditures for higher education will decline. But what had been the most expensive service in the portfolio of many state governments (along with highways) may take a lesser portion of state revenues and leave greater slices for other programs.

STATE TAX SYSTEMS

The strength of state tax systems will continue to rest on sales and income taxes. At the present time 46 of the states collect a levy on personal or corporate incomes and 45 a tax on retail sales. Expressed in other terms, income and sales taxes each account for about 31 percent of state tax revenues. The sales tax was the favorite vehicle for revenue increases from the end of World War II to the late 1950s. From then until the present, however, the personal income tax has carried the burden of increasing demands. Between 1958 and 1974, individual income taxes have risen from 10 to 23 percent of state tax revenues. Local governments will not wither away as taxing and service-providing entities, but they will remain weak. Local property tax collections per capita have increased less than the collections of the major state taxes. State tax collections were increasing by 656 percent between 1950 and 1973, while local property taxes increased by 529 percent. An increasing number of states now permit localities to tax retail sales and personal incomes. However, the rates of these taxes remain low and many localities do not take advantage of their options. During 1973, income and sales taxes provided only 9 percent of local tax revenue. Moreover, only state governments retain a capacity to tax their entire economies. Especially in metropolitan areas, states have the advantage over local governments in imposing their levies across municipal boundaries. If any government below the level of Washington is to extract revenues from an entire urban area—without foundering on the miasma of metropolitan reform—it will be state governments. Those who look to a local-national axis for the development of major new programs should recognize that the financial weaknesses and distractions of local and national governments are responsible for the recent surge of state activity.

How high can all state taxes go? This question requires a crystal ball. Governments in western nations outside of the United States extract greater portions of available resources than governments in the United States. During World War II, all levels of government in the United States drew about 52 percent out of the Gross National Product. During 1973 American government spending accounted for a mere 32 percent of GNP—even while fighting another war and helping several allies finance their own. There is room in the economy for higher state taxes. Many low-income states surpass the high-income states in the resources they extract from their private sectors. State taxes are likely to reflect officials' assertiveness and the constraints in their political cultures, rather than the operation of irreversible economic laws.

THE COSTS OF INTERNATIONAL COMMITMENTS

How nice it would be if the nation's international activities became less expensive and allowed us to spend the Pentagon's billions on our own social and economic problems. There was a short while in the late

1960s when serious analysts calculated the fiscal bonus to be released by withdrawal from Vietnam. The optimistic predictions went from $10 billion annually in the early 1970s to $35-$40 billion annually by the mid-1970s.[1] In fact, the percentage of the national budget allocated to defense dropped from 44 in 1968 to slightly less than 25 in 1976. Despite some talk in that direction, however, the United States had not withdrawn from the world in the aftermath of Vietnam. The United States was dominant in the calculus of leaders in every region. Washington's financial outlays for military and economic assistance were heaviest in the Middle East. Israel, Egypt, and Jordan each viewed the United States as crucial. We may all wish for peace, but it is too early to base any policy forecasts on its coming. State governments will continue to pay for social programs that might receive Federal aid in a more benign world.

The oil embargo that followed the 1973 war in the Middle East was a feature of American international commitments that made itself felt in state policy making. Individual states preceded Washington in countering the energy crisis with lowered highway speed limits. As the shortage of energy moved from the crisis period to assume long-term chronic dimensions, however, we saw another side to state policy: the competition between energy producers and consumers to assure for their own residents and industries an adequate share of the nation's fuel resources. This was a time for Federal action to coordinate domestic and international interests, but what emerged from Washington seemed more like vacillation between conflicting pressures than any clear or consistent energy policy.

URBAN AREAS

As increasing numbers move into metropolitan areas they will continue to manifest both considerable health and illness in our economic system. Income levels will rise in urban areas while slums persist and—according to some measurements—spread. The cities will continue as the locales of our most complex and expensive domestic programs. Also, barring any radical change in social preferences and patterns of investment (e.g., population dispersal, rural industrialization, lots of new towns), the urban areas will show both a surplus of governments whose activities are uncoordinated and demands to create even more local governments in suburban and core areas. In all probability, the states' attention will focus increasingly on urban residents. Below the level of Washington, the states are likely to have the only governments with revenue mechanisms that cover whole metropolitan areas. State services can remain oblivious to intra-urban disparities in the taxable property of local jurisdictions. State parks, universities, and hospitals can serve a whole metropolis without the central city or a suburb feeling it is paying the whole cost of someone else's service. Urban branches of state universities may expand their programs at faster rates than more established rural campuses. Already the urban universities provide a wide range of academic programs. State aids to local governments will also increase. The aids will reflect the greater strength of the state taxing powers. Especially where state constitutions make it difficult for local governments to tax personal incomes and retail sales, the cities may rely on state aids for an increasing portion of their revenues.

The continuing reapportionment of state legislatures should add to the pressures for state governments to help the cities. With the Supreme Court's landmark decision of 1962, the principle of "one man, one vote" is a dominant theme in state assemblies. Increasing urban populations will mean an increasing proportion of legislators from urban areas. There are several unanswered questions about the behavior of these new representatives. In some states the suburbs and not the central cities benefit most from reapportionment. Suburban Republicans may vote with rural Republicans against central city Democrats. In some states an increase in urban legislators may only mean more bitter struggles between representatives from different cities, or between the representatives of different social groups in the cities. However, results from Georgia should encourage urban residents. After court-ordered reapportionment, the heavily urbanized districts of Georgia went from 6 to 57 seats in the lower house and from 1 to 21 seats in the upper house.[2] The Atlanta metropolitan area went from 13 representatives and 4 senators to 46 representatives and 13 senators. There were also changes in the personal and political attributes of legislators. The average age dropped from 51 to 35 years; the number of college-educated members of the lower house went from 69 to 85; the number of blacks from 1 to 11; and the Republicans from 2 to 23. Since reapportionment, urban legislators appear more often in leadership positions: as chairpersons and vice-chairpersons of key committees.[3] Georgia's urban legislators are voting together more often—and winning more roll calls—

than before reapportionment.[4] The urban victories occur in areas that are important for city residents: taxation, local government powers, state aids, and the regulation of business and labor. A study of states all over the country finds the largest increases in state aids to cities coming in those states having greatest changes in apportionment.[5] Perhaps it is not the Supreme Court itself that is producing these changes. The increase in urban voting noted for Georgia legislators began prior to the state's reapportionment. The Court's decisions may reflect more basic changes in the society's awareness of urban affairs. Whatever the root cause of policy changes already observed, many cities seem likely to profit from increased voting power in state legislatures.[6]

HIGHER EDUCATION

There should be a lessening of enrollment pressures on state colleges and universities. Projections made by the National Center for Educational Statistics show a growth rate of 10 percent from 1973 to 1983. This compares with a rate of 153 percent for 1960-1973. Behind these estimates is the discovery that the percentage of college-age youth taking advantage of higher education has ended its period of dramatic increase. This figure went from 33 to 47 between 1960 and 1973, but is thought likely to increase by only one more percentage point by 1983. While the details of these projections are subject to some dispute, their principal message finds support in recent experience.

Public spending for higher education is already flattening its increase. The period 1960–1961 to 1970–1971 saw growth of 362 percent in state tax funds to operate higher education. This means an increase of about 70 percent every 2 years! In the most recent 2-year period, however, the growth was only 15 percent. This does not promise cutbacks in state budgets for higher education. It only means a reduction in the annual growth rate of higher education spending. No massive "post higher education bonus" will be available for other state programs. New or rapidly growing institutions may take advantage of the lessened pressure to flesh out their programs. Others may increase their teacher-student ratios. As inflation continues (and no prognosis can rely on its halt), states will pay more for new construction and faculty salaries. Higher education will continue as a big lump in state budgets.

As enrollments peak, however, other programs may increase their percentage take of state funds.

PUBLIC WELFARE

Welfare is an important and controversial area of state policy whose recent history blurs rather than clarifies its future. State expenditures for public welfare have shown the greatest increases in the 1968–1973 period, with a growth rate about twice that of total spending. The factors responsible for this spurt include an increased awareness of program benefits among potential clients (brought about partly by state-financed public relations activities), as well as increases in the prices and coverage of medical assistance for the needy, and some program shifts from local to state levels. It is particularly difficult to make projections in the welfare field, given the record for dramatic increases in the prices of medical care and the fickle character of public attitudes with respect to the support of poor citizens.[7] With these reservations, however, the advent of a greater Federal role should seem to permit a stabilization of state efforts in welfare. As noted in Chapter 5, there is now a presumption of Federal leadership in public assistance programs for the aged, blind, and disabled. State governments may continue to supplement these programs with their own sums; however, there seems to be minimum incentives for state supplements, especially in the case of low-income states with a history of welfare conservatism. Indeed, the advent of the new arrangements in 1974 brought about a decline in the share of state spending going to welfare from 18 to 17 percent and an increase in the share of Federal expenditures going to welfare from 30 to 31 percent. Estimating the Federal budget for 1977, one sees an additional increase of 3 percent in the share of Federal spending going to welfare.

Where does this leave the state governments? With a respectable place in American politics. If present trends continue, the states will assume an increasing share of financial and administrative tasks. Policy makers at all levels of government should see the states as strong partners in the Federal structure. The states do not deserve a tattered reputation. They have problems, to be sure. Just as some states compile enviable records for certain programs, others bring shame to the whole country. For much that is good and bad about the states, it is proper to divide their responsibility with local and national governments. No active citizen should be content with the states as they are. Yet no intelligent citizen should plan to improve the country without making an important place for the states.

A PERSPECTIVE AND A MODEST PROPOSAL

At the conclusion of this book, a reader might expect detailed recommendations to push forward on the strong backs of state governments. Yet our major task is analysis and evaluation, not prescription. For a book that concedes the ambivalence of state governments in its title, it would be incongruous to wind up with any wholesale recommendation. There are problems as well as accomplishments and opportunities in the recent history of the American states. General policy recommendations for state governments require appropriate hedges concerning a host of issues. Given the wide variations from one state to another, it is safer to make recommendations for certain classes of states than for all of them together. The only general recommendations that are appropriate lead us to credit many states for their accomplishments and to be wary of excessive reliance on the national-local axis. Detailed advice requires focused discussions about each level of state activity.

Even though no detailed recommendations emerge from this book, it offers a perspective that can lead to a modest proposal. The perspective has two parts:

1 States differ from one another in their reliability to conduct creditable programs.

2 The Federal government can support and encourage the performance of state governments and shares responsibility for the failures in state programs.

Some states are generally creative and responsible across a wide range of public services, while others seldom earn citations for creativity or responsibility. For most of the states, however, there is considerable variation from one kind of policy to another. They do not benefit from complementary mixtures of economic wealth, public-minded cultures, honest and imaginative politicians that produce admirable programs across the board; but they do have the right mixtures of personalities, traditions, and statutes that benefit limited policy sectors. Oklahoma stands out in public assistance, Mississippi in tax policy, and Alabama in old-age assistance.

While other books stress the benefits provided to the states by the Federal government, it is unfair to stop at the commendation of Washington. The Federal government has let down state officials on numerous occasions, and at other times it has encouraged the states to offer undesirable programs. The most glaring case of negative incentives appears in the formula for public assistance grants that for many years encouraged low-income states to make small monthly payments to their welfare recipients. The Federal government helped produce the glaring inequities in welfare programs that are commonly laid at the feet of the state governments.

It is not yet clear how the Federal government will exercise its new responsibilities in the welfare field. There is a potential for much greater equality of benefits from state to state, at least in the programs where the national government has accepted a leading role. Even in these, however, a successful reform will require a persistence of Congressional and administrative concern for the poor, against the competition for resources from other services and the notoriously unstable nature of support for welfare.

In the field of higher education, the residents of Michigan, California, Wisconsin, North Carolina, and other states with well-developed colleges have long provided below-cost education to residents of New York, New Jersey, Connecticut, and Pennsylvania. For many years these well-to-do states neglected their residents' needs for public higher education. Even though they do more now than in the past, they remain low-spenders in the field and a disproportionate number of their students go elsewhere for their education. The Federal government has an obvious responsibility here: either Federal scholarships that residents of the lagging states can use elsewhere, Federal grants to help the well-situated states pay for the education they provide to residents of other states, or Federal incentives for the lagging states to do more for their own residents.

In the field of highway safety, many states required vehicle inspection but felt that they were making small progress against a basic problem of poorly designed vehicles. It was not until 1968 that the

Federal government entered the field with safety standards and enforcement against the manufacturers.

In the urban field, the national government pursues a variety of
programs that offer direct assistance to municipal governments and
private organizations, but has avoided any concerted effort to induce
urban-oriented programs out of state governments. Contrary to much
current thought, state governments are not the cities' natural enemies.
Now we finally have Federal guarantees of equity in legislative apportionment. We have also seen increases in both state and Federal aid for
the largest cities, as well as increases in the direct provision of state
services in urban areas. These appear to be better methods for channeling
resources into urban areas than the integration of all local governments
in metropolitan areas. They avoid problems of local jealousies and the
parochialisms of suburb and ghetto. The direct provision of state services in the urban area may not avoid all interurban problems, but it
does rely on state policy makers whose base of support is outside the
immediate environs of bickering neighbors.

The advent of Federal revenue-sharing signaled a dramatic but
partial change in the Federal-state relationship. Certain supporters of
revenue-sharing wanted to extend the concept further. They would
increase the sums available under revenue-sharing that states could spend
with relative freedom, but decrease or curtail equivalent portions of
grants-in-aid for specific programs. To some observers, this would be
too much of a good thing. While welcoming the resources and the
freedom of revenue-sharing, they do not want to give up all the specifica-
tions of existing grants or to rely on 50 state governments for continuation of programs now covered by the grants. The Alabama syndrome is
still a lively and threatening feature of the Federal system. The
Milwaukee Journal of February 22, 1971, reported the following events
in connection with Alabama's use of the Safe Streets Act, a grant program enacted in advance of revenue-sharing but with provisions allowing
considerable freedom of state action.

1 A $200,000 officer education program was used largely to send
the sons of high-ranking public safety department officials to college,
with scholarships and pay of up to $6,000 per year.

2 A newspaper editor, a television news reporter, and his father—
none with law enforcement experience—formed a corporation called
Criminal Justice Systems, Inc. which in the absence of competitive

bidding was paid $91,570 in advance to prepare the 1971 report of the Alabama Law Enforcement Planning Agency.

   3   The State's Attorney General's Office was paid $11,950 to produce a law enforcement officers' handbook. Most of the grant went in consultant fees to assistant attorneys general. One drew $2,250. Almost 18 months after the payment, however, no book had been produced.

When President Nixon tried to follow his revenue-sharing success with further extensions of the principle (called special revenue-sharing and requiring decreases in certain grants-in-aid), supporters of individual grant programs worked to block his proposal. Thus, there has been a continuation of grants-in-aid along with revenue-sharing. Indeed, annual Federal spending under traditional concepts of grants-in-aid increased by almost $20 billion and 55 percent in the first 5 years of revenue-sharing.

Our modest proposal would continue this ambivalent treatment of the states: a bit of control and a bit of free resources to be used at their discretion. Ideally, the Federal government should treat the states differently, allowing more discretion where the situation permits.

There is precedent for such a policy in the case of voting rights: only states with a history of overt racial discrimination are held to the highest standards of behavior. For other kinds of policy, the Federal government should offer material inducements as well as sanctions in a differential manner.

There is some indication that Federal administrators "loosen up" their supervision informally under the existing grants-in-aid programs as a program matures and as the officials of certain states gain the respect of the Federal agency. Yet the autonomy of the states does not become complete. And as in the case of other informal arrangements, what is gained in state discretion can be lost without any state recourse to clear standards or due process.

What is preferred to the present informality of state discretion—or to the wholesale devolution of autonomy represented by some proposals for revenue sharing—is a more systematic arrangement that seeks to identify the areas of state strength and weakness, then rewards strength and induces improvement in weakness. This is easier said than done. Before any concrete proposals can be offered, it is necessary to have more information about state strengths and weaknesses than is presently available, and to be certain that the proposals offered are not vulnerable to the deadening attack of political unfeasibility. Of prime importance is the information. With more adequate data about state programs in each sector of public service, it may be possible to design programs with sufficiently attractive incentives to produce the political coalitions that are necessary.

There is already a good beginning of policy-relevant information about the states. Political scientists and other social scientists have become increasingly sophisticated in their descriptions of state economies, political institutions, and public services.[8] We know a great deal about the nature of state policies and the economic conditions that are generally associated with each kind of policy. We can determine which states produce the more or less admirable programs in each field of policy, and which states do better or less well than expected on the basis of their resources. As information like this becomes more complete in its coverage of state programs, it will be possible to identify the states that should be left free to use Federal funds unhindered in certain fields of policy and the states that should receive inducements and supervision to upgrade their programs. The tasks of policy assessment will not be easy. There will be debates over appropriate definitions for each field of policy, measurements that reflect accurately the important features in each field, the standards that will determine whether a state is left on its own to use Federal money or is subject to Federal supervision, and the kinds of inducements and supervision that are appropriate for each kind of policy. It will also be necessary to design standards and mechanisms for reestablishing Federal control— once it has been loosened and state agencies have strayed onto the low road.

Some may say these recommendations will give too much power to the Federal government and carry even further the subordination of the states. Yet others should applaud the therapy that states will receive. Well-designed inducements can lead state agencies out of Federal tutelage and to a condition where they use Federal funds according to their own discretion. The proposal is offered from a perspective that respects the accomplishments and potentials of state governments, but also recognizes that economic and political problems in some of the states deprive their citizens of important opportunities for public services. In order to preserve the variety and the creativity that state governments offer to all of us we should pursue a multifaceted program that recognizes sectors of strength and weakness, and deals with each in an appropriate manner.

NOTES

1 Henry S. Reuss, *Revenue-Sharing: Crutch or Catalyst for State and Local Governments* (New York: Praeger, 1970), p. 83.

2 Thomas R. Dye, "The Impact of Reapportionment on the Characteristics of Georgia Legislators," and "The Impact of Reapportionment on the Representation Afforded Various Constituencies in Georgia," University of Georgia, mimeo. The definition of "heavily urbanized" districts are those with 90–100 percent of their residents living in areas defined as "urban" by the U.S. Bureau of the Census.

3 Brett Hawkins and Cheryl Whelchel, "Reapportionment and Urban Representation in Legislative Influence Positions: The Case of Georgia," *Urban Affairs Quarterly* 3 (March 1968), pp. 69–80.

4 Ira Sharkansky, "Reapportionment and Roll Call Voting: The Case of the Georgia Legislature," *Social Science Quarterly* 51 (June 1970), pp. 130–137.

5 See H. George Frederickson and Yong Hyo Cho, "Legislative Reapportionment and Public Policy in the American States," a paper given at the 1970 meeting of the American Political Science Association Los Angeles.

6 A number of studies published in the 1960s compared the policies offered by the best- and worst-apportioned states prior to the reapportionments that occurred in the 1960s. See their citation in Sharkansky, "Reapportionment. . . ." This earlier scholarship finds little differences in the policies of the two groups of states. The findings should discourage any expectation that *wholesale and immediate* policy changes will occur as a direct result of reapportionment. However, my own research in Georgia and the findings of Frederickson and Cho (see note 5) suggest that substantial, if gradual, improvements in the states' urban policies will follow the apportionment doctrines of the Federal courts.

7 On this point see Frances Fox Piven and Richard Cloward, *Regulating the Poor: The Functions of Public Welfare* (New York: Pantheon, 1971).

8 See Herbert Jacob and Kenneth N. Vines, *Politics in the American States: A Comparative Analysis,* 2d ed. (Boston: Little, Brown, 1971).

Index

Individual states are indexed only if they are the subject of detailed comment.